Iran after
Khomeini

THE WASHINGTON PAPERS

... intended to meet the need for an authoritative, yet prompt, public appraisal of the major developments in world affairs.

President, CSIS: David M. Abshire

Series Editor: Walter Laqueur

Director of Publications: Nancy B. Eddy

Managing Editor: Donna R. Spitler

MANUSCRIPT SUBMISSION

The Washington Papers and Praeger Publishers welcome inquiries concerning manuscript submissions. Please include with your inquiry a curriculum vitae, synopsis, table of contents, and estimated manuscript length. Manuscript length must be between 120 and 200 double-spaced typed pages. All submissions will be peer reviewed. Submissions to *The Washington Papers* should be sent to *The Washington Papers*; The Center for Strategic and International Studies; 1800 K Street NW; Suite 400; Washington, DC 20006. Book proposals should be sent to Praeger Publishers; One Madison Avenue; New York, NY 10010.

The Washington Papers/156

Iran after Khomeini

Shireen T. Hunter

Foreword by David D. Newsom

Published with The Center for
Strategic and International Studies
Washington, D.C.

New York
Westport, Connecticut
London

Library of Congress Cataloging-in-Publication Data

Hunter, Shireen.
    Iran after Khomeini / Shireen T. Hunter.
        p. cm. — (The Washington papers, ISSN 0278-937X ; 156)
    "Published with The Center for Strategic and International
Studies, Washington, D.C."
    Includes bibliographical references and index.
    ISBN 0-275-94293-7 (cloth). — ISBN 0-275-94292-9 (paper)
    1. Iran—History—1979-   I. Center for Strategic
and International Studies.   II. Title.   III. Series.
DS318'.8.H865   1992
955.05'4—dc20   92-2522

The *Washington Papers* are written under the auspices of The Center
for Strategic and International Studies (CSIS) and published
with CSIS by Praeger Publishers. The views expressed in these papers
are those of the authors and not necessarily those of the Center.

British Library Cataloging in Publication data is available.

Library of Congress Catalog Card Number: 92-2522
ISBN: 0-275-94293-7 (cloth)
        0-275-94292-9 (paper)

First published in 1992

Praeger Publishers, One Madison Avenue, New York, NY 10010
An imprint of Greenwood Publishing Group, Inc.

Printed in the United States of America

The paper used in this book complies with the Permanent
Paper Standard issued by the National Information Standards
Organization (Z39.48-1984).

10   9   8   7   6   5   4   3   2   1

Contents

Foreword   vii

About the Author   xi

Summary   xiii

Introduction   1

1. **Constitutional and Political Issues**   6

     Iran's Political System and Its Cultural
         Foundations in 1979   6
     Iran's Islamic Constitution and Its Cultural
         and Ideological Basis   14
     Developments Following Constitutional Reform   32

2. **The Military Establishment: Adapting to
     Peacetime**   46

     Background and Developments since
         the Revolution   46
     The Role of the Military in Iranian Society
         and Politics   50
     The Size of the Military Establishment   53

3. The Economy: From Boom to Bust to What?   56

    Weaknesses of the Shah's Economic Policy   56
    Ideological Confusion: Impediment to
        Economic Planning and Development   58
    Islamic Economics: Is It Possible?   61
    The First Economic Development Plan   65
    Current Characteristics of the Economy   67
    Economic Prospects: Challenges and Assets   74
    Rafsanjani's Economic Policies and Plans   80

4. Culture and Society: Toward a New
    Islamo-Nationalist Synthesis?   92

    Relegitimizing Iranianism   94
    Rehabilitating Iran's Literary Figures   95
    Encouraging the Arts, Publishing, and
        Electronic Media   95
    Islamization of Education: Challenges of
        Modernity   98
    Research and Development   100

5. Foreign Relations: Continuity and Change   101

    Iran's Foreign Relations in 1979   102
    Developments after the Revolution   106
    The Transitional Period   109
    1981–1984: Radical Ascendancy and the
        Export of Revolution   112
    1984–1988: Continued Tug of War, Fluctuation,
        and Creeping Realism   114
    The Ayatollah Khomeini's Death and the
        Rafsanjani Presidency   121
    Iraq's Invasion of Kuwait: New Opportunities
        and Challenges for Iranian Foreign Policy 126

Conclusions and Outlook   139

Notes   145

Index   156

Foreword

For the United States, the revolution in Iran in 1979 represented both trauma and challenge. Through its sponsorship of hostage-taking and terrorism, the new leadership in Tehran became a hated symbol for much of the U.S. public. Yet Washington, with its global reach, could not – and cannot – ignore Iran, lying as it does in a central position on the southern Asian land mass. In Asia, only China is contiguous with more states. Today, with the creation of the Commonwealth of Independent States, Iran has common borders with seven countries: Pakistan, Afghanistan, Turkmenistan, Azerbaijan, Armenia, Turkey, and Iraq. Five more nations of special interest to the United States lie in close proximity across the Gulf: Kuwait, Saudi Arabia, Qatar, the United Arab Emirates, and Oman.

In varying degrees, Iranian cultural and religious influence has spread and affected not only each of its neighbors, but nations of the Islamic world beyond. Although significant differences exist between Shi'a Iran and the predominantly Sunni nations of the rest of the Muslim world, the revolutionary message of the Ayatollah Khomeini – including Tehran's strong opposition to peace with Israel—has been heard from Kuala Lumpur to Rabat. Iran is already reported to be vying with Turkey and Pakistan for influence in the Muslim republics of Central Asia.

In the Iran-Iraq War, Washington came to realize that a total Iranian defeat was not in the interest of the United States or of stability in the region. In the Gulf War, the United States was quietly appreciative of Iranian restraint. Despite such setbacks as the Iran-contra affair, some gradual increase in official contacts between Washington and Tehran would appear to be in the interest of both countries. As Shireen Hunter points out in this timely and perceptive monograph that follows, President George Bush has himself noted on several occasions that Iran should not be forever considered as a pariah.

Yet the path to normalization of relations between the two countries will not be an easy one. On both sides, the past stands in the way of any dramatic change in the relationship. Political leaders in both countries remain vulnerable to criticism from publics that are not yet ready to forget recent history and from opponents who would exploit that vulnerability. Tehran's past insults and provocations will not be quickly forgotten in the United States. In Iran neither the enmity against "the great Satan" of the past nor the sentiments born of the revolution can be quickly suppressed. Although President Ali Akbar Hashemi Rafsanjani has sought to steer a more moderate course, many in Iran's leadership still regard the United States as the source of previous humiliation and as an enemy to the success of the revolution.

Yet, positive signs exist on the horizon. The ending—for the United States, at least—of the hostage crisis in Lebanon removes one major barrier to normal ties. The process of claims settlement under the Algiers accord continues at The Hague. Some trade has been resumed.

During such a period of gradual restoration, policymakers and public alike need to remain objectively informed as to what is happening in each country. Writing from her unique professional perspective, Shireen Hunter helps to bring this about.

David D. Newsom

Hugh and Winifred B. Cumming Memorial Professor
of International Relations, University of Virginia
Former Under Secretary of State for Political Affairs,
1978–1981

About the Author

Shireen T. Hunter is deputy director of the Middle East Program at the Center for Strategic and International Studies. Her publications include *OPEC and the Third World: Politics of Aid* (1984), *The Politics of Islamic Revivalism: Diversity and Unity* (1986), and *Iran and the World: Continuity in a Revolutionary Decade* (1990). She has contributed chapters to numerous edited volumes, and her articles have appeared in such journals as *Foreign Affairs, Foreign Policy, SAIS Review, Current History, Third World Quarterly, OPEC Review, Middle East Journal, Middle East International,* and *Relazioni Internazionali.*

Summary

This volume analyzes Iran's internal developments following the death, on June 5, 1989, of the Ayatollah Ruhollah Khomeini, founder of the Islamic Republic of Iran. Placing post-Khomeini developments in appropriate historical context, it also addresses the changes that have occurred in Iran's foreign policy since that time.

The study endeavors to explain, and clarify, the long-term implications of post-Khomeini developments for Iran's future direction in both domestic and foreign policy. It emphasizes how Iran's internal developments and recent international developments, most notably the changes in the Soviet Union and the Persian Gulf, have affected the course of Iran's foreign policy.

The author examines the transition of power after the Ayatollah Khomeini, as well as constitutional reforms and their significance for Iran's political future. From the experience of the past three years emerge three long-term trends with far-reaching, but still unclear, political implications for Iran:

• Rising statism and the growing subordination of religious principles and considerations to the political necessities of state and regime survival.

• Fledgling movement toward some form of Islamic reformation and the beginning of a move toward a gradual separation of religion and politics. Especially important in this respect has been the constitutional amendment eliminating the requirement of the 1979 Islamic constitution for the next supreme religious leader to be a source of emulation. This trend is still in its very early stages, however, and its final outcome is not clear.

• Intensified pragmatism in Iranian politics, despite the persistence of powerful pockets of radical tendencies. The primary causes of this phenomenon have been the failure of the radicals' economic policies, the rising popular dissatisfaction with continued economic hardship, and the excessive rigor of the radicals' moral code.

Despite these encouraging trends, constitutional reforms have not resolved some of the underlying problems and contradictions of the Islamic regime. These problems derive from the nature of Islamic law and the Shi'a jurisprudence and political philosophy, as well as from the notion of the Velayat-e-Faqih. These reforms have not led to effective instruments for resolving the intraregime political differences or for settling divergent opinions on the interpretation of Islamic principles and legal and philosophical concepts. This failure, the study notes, somewhat clouds the regime's future, despite the smooth transition of power after the Ayatollah Khomeini's death. To prevent future problems, other legal and political reforms are necessary.

This volume discusses difficulties encountered by the Iranian authorities in attempting to restore law and order, enhance the professionalism and efficiency of the Iranian bureaucracy, and integrate Iran's military forces, notably the regular armed forces and the Revolutionary Guards. Without essential reforms in all these fields, Iran's chances of resolving its economic problems and successfully completing its economic reconstruction will be severely undermined.

In an analysis of Iran's economic challenges and prospects, the author notes that Iran's considerable natural, financial, and human resources – both within the country and abroad among the Iranian exile communities – provide it with significant assets, which if properly utilized could go a long way in resolving problems. Iran's problems derive mainly from significant political barriers – notably the radical sabotage – in the way of harnessing and utilizing these resources and from the enormous dimensions of its economic reconstruction needs. Yet the Iranian government's determination to make difficult economic decisions and to undertake monetary and other reforms, including measures to privatize the economy, warrants some optimism about its ability to overcome these barriers. Ultimately, however, Iran's economic success depends on the government's ability to resolve existing political problems, which is vital to restoring the confidence in Iran's future of both the Iranians and foreign countries.

On the cultural front, this volume notes a steady reassertion of Iranianism, a rehabilitation of Iran's cultural heritage, and a trend toward a new synthesis of the Islamic and Iranian nationalist dimensions of Iran's culture. These are positive developments with potentially significant implications for Iran's future political orientation. On the domestic front, an Islamic-nationalist synthesis would facilitate national reconciliation in Iran that is indispensable to realizing Iran's economic and political aspirations. On the foreign policy front, a reassertion of Iranianism, coupled with the rise of statism, has already led to an approach that is more nationalist – in the sense that Iran's national interest has been given priority over other considerations.

The impact of this development was clearly evident in the way Iran responded to Iraq's invasion of Kuwait, the Persian Gulf war, and its aftermath. Iran's other foreign policy moves – ranging from its actively courting the Persian Gulf Arab governments and establishing relations with other Arab states to its improving ties with the West and releasing the Western hostages – reflect this growing nationalist, pragmatist trend.

Yet the influence of the radical ideologues on Iran's foreign policy has not been totally eliminated. This radical influence continues to hamper Iran's diplomacy and its rapid and complete reintegration in the international community. Given the new and difficult choices that the recent international and regional changes have posed for the Iranian leadership, however, Iran's handling of its foreign relations in the last three years has shown an enhanced level of sophistication and diplomatic skill.

This volume illustrates the very long distance that Iran has yet to travel on its way to economic reconstruction, political stability and maturity, and international rehabilitation. But Iran's record of the last three years — its leadership's handling of the transition to the post-Khomeini era, the enormous tasks of economic reconstruction, and the Iranian response to dramatic international events — warrant a greater degree of optimism about Iran's future prospects than has been the case for a long time.

Iran after Khomeini

Introduction

The Ayatollah Ruhollah Khomeini – the man who brought down the shah, ended a 2,500-year tradition of monarchy in Iran, turned three decades of U.S.-Iranian amity into bitter enmity, and for 10 years was Iran's uncontested leader – died June 5, 1989. With his passing, a turbulent episode in Iran's millenarian history ended.

Three years after his departure, Iran's political future remains uncertain. And so does the fate of the Ayatollah Khomeini's vision of an ideal and united Islamic community.

It is clear, however, that no one in the near future will be able to replace Ayatollah Khomeini in Iran or in the Muslim world. It is also evident that his model of an Islamic government is ill equipped to deal with Iran's problems of economic reconstruction and social and political consolidation. It is a model that cannot cope with the challenges of a rapidly changing and increasingly interdependent world. It is equally clear that his Islamic vision in its purest form is incompatible with some of Iran's historical and cultural characteristics and with the preferences of many Iranians.

It follows, therefore, that the Islamic regime must reform. It must adapt to Iran's fundamental realities. It also needs to equip itself better to deal with external challenges.

1

Indeed, Iran's leaders recognized the need to adapt to national and international environments even before Ayatollah Khomeini's death.

For 10 years, Iran's foreign relations were greatly influenced by the Ayatollah Khomeini's vision of and quest for an ideal Islamic political order, for which Iran paid heavy human and material costs. Moreover, Iran's efforts to export its revolution to mostly unreceptive audiences led to countermeasures by other states that weakened Iran and led to its isolation and loss of international standing. Thus, during the last years of Ayatollah Khomeini's life, Iran was forced to abandon the blind pursuit of this revolutionary and utopian vision in deed if not in word.

More than anything else, the eight-year war with Iraq revealed to Iranians how unrealistic this vision was and how heavy its costs were. True, Iran did not start the war, but did prolong it by refusing to accept a negotiated peace. Although Iran's grievances against the international community for failing to condemn Iraqi aggression were justified, its inflexibility forced the international community into a position that cost Iran heavily. The buildup of international resistance to Iran culminated in the U.S.-Iran military confrontation in the Persian Gulf and in the devastating events of the summer of 1988, which forced Iran to accept peace from a position of weakness.

In Iran these events generated the most intense debate since the revolution on its foreign policy and especially on the devastating consequences of an unrealistic diplomacy. This debate has greatly abated but has not ended. Depending on the external circumstances, especially on developments in Iran's immediate surroundings, it could be reignited.

To focus solely, however, on the shortcomings of the Islamic regime and its failure to realize Ayatollah Khomeini's Islamic vision would present an inaccurate picture of Iran's Islamic experience. For the sake of accuracy and balance, the regime's successes should also be noted. Moreover, the Islamic regime's record should be compared with those of other Middle Eastern and South Asian countries and not judged according to the standards of economically advanced countries.

The Islamic regime's greatest success has been its ability to survive for more than 10 years despite internal and external challenges that have included a devastating foreign war, guerrilla warfare by ethnic minorities and other opposition groups often armed and financed from abroad, and economic and military embargoes.

The regime has also maintained Iran's territorial integrity, a significant degree of national unity, and some degree of economic activity in the face of great odds. Given the devastation that Iran has suffered and the cost of a lost decade in economic and social development, these achievements may not be great. They reflect, however, the resilience and survival strength of both the Iranian nation and government. They also belie the view of Iran as an inherently unstable national unit, a hodgepodge of quarreling ethnic groups.

The Islamic regime has also survived the passing of its founder, despite expectations of a quick collapse following the Ayatollah Khomeini's death. Here, too, the regime's success has been partial. The Islamic leadership has maintained enough unity for a smooth transition of power, but internal differences persist. The regime has not yet devised effective mechanisms to mediate these differences and to reach decisions that the whole government will follow. This situation in the past three years has slowed reform and economic recovery as well as Iran's international rehabilitation. It must be noted, however, that the Islamic regime's internal differences are not merely the result of disagreements among different factions. Rather, they reflect deep-rooted national dichotomies relating to such fundamental issues as the nature of Iran's national identity, the tension between the requirements of modernization and the desire to maintain cultural purity and spirituality, and the tension between economic efficiency and social justice. None of these issues were openly discussed in the past.

It is a positive phenomenon of the past few years, however, that these issues have been openly discussed in the
Iranian press, Parliament, and society at large. Under ideal
circumstances, the scope of this debate and the range of its
participants would be broadened, ultimately leading to a
new and broad-based national consensus on these matters
and on the best means of achieving a balanced approach to
them.

If such were to happen, then what has been called Iran's
"chronic factionalism" could be transformed into an orderly
pluralism. Even if ultimately successful, however, this process is likely to be long, even turbulent. The outlines of a
new national consensus are not clearly defined, but some of
its necessary ingredients are already obvious. It is also
clear that the Islamic regime's survival and future success
lie in its ability to reconcile these national dichotomies and
to develop a new national consensus.

Some of the latest trends in Iran, including efforts at
national reconciliation, provide some reason for optimism
that it will succeed in mitigating—if not completely resolving—its national dichotomies. If successful, this development could usher in a new era of national healing and reconciliation among Iranians, who have been deeply divided
since the revolution, thus leading to greater national unity.

Indeed, national reconciliation seems to be one of President Ali Akbar Hashemi Rafsanjani's priorities. His realistic and pragmatic outlook, his political skills, and his style
of governing are reasons to be cautiously optimistic about
his chances for success. The problems that he has to overcome are enormous, however; popular expectations of him
are high, and his opponents are bent on sabotaging his
efforts.

Given Iran's sensitive strategic position and the un-
leashing of new forces around it because of the changes in
the Soviet Union and the Persian Gulf War, external factors
will play very important roles in determining the regime's
fortunes and Iran's national fate.

Iraq's invasion of Kuwait on August 2, 1990, and the

introduction of foreign, especially massive U.S., military forces into the Persian Gulf, leading to the outbreak of hostilities on January 16, 1991, have dramatically changed the external setting of Iranian politics. The Persian Gulf crisis has had positive short-term effects on Iran, but its long-term consequences could prove to be very negative. Much will depend on Iraq's political future — whether there will be significant territorial changes, permanent stationing of foreign forces, and drastic realignments in the region. Be that as it may, the crisis has once more demonstrated Iran's acute and historic vulnerability to events beyond its control.

This volume explores the directions the Islamic regime and, more important, the Iranian society and nation are likely to take in the 1990s. The study begins with a brief historical survey of Iran's political institutions, its sociocultural traits, and its economic and military conditions, as well as its foreign policy orientation at the time of the revolution. It follows with a summary of the political, social, and economic changes the Islamic revolution introduced. Together the survey and summary serve as benchmarks against which to measure the changes and reforms of the last three years. They also provide a basis for sketching the potential directions of Iran's domestic evolution and its foreign relations.

1

Constitutional and Political Issues

**Iran's Political System and Its
Cultural Foundations in 1979**

At the time of the Islamic revolution, Iran was nominally a constitutional monarchy. The legal basis of this system was the 1906 constitution and the supplementary constitution of 1907 that was adopted after the constitutional revolution of 1905–1906. The constitution was later amended to accommodate Reza Pahlavi's assumption of Iran's throne and the newly formed Pahlavi dynasty's replacement of the Qajar dynasty.[1] The Pahlavis largely ignored the provisions of the 1906 constitution, however, thus sowing the seeds of a profound political and cultural discord among Iranians.

To understand this phenomenon requires understanding the nature of the 1906 constitution. It was based on a political compromise between the two groups that cooperated in Iran's constitutional movement – between the secular-nationalists and the Islamic forces. The secular-nationalist influence was reflected in the constitution through the incorporation of liberal-democratic ideals in respect to both the organization of the government and the rights of the Iranian people.[2] The Islamic influence was reflected in two decisive ways. First, Article 5 of the constitution stipulated

6

that no legislation should contravene Islamic law. To ensure this, it provided that five eminent and recognized Muslim clerics should always sit in the parliament. Second, personal freedoms were limited to those activities that were congruent with Islamic morality and did not undermine Iran's Islamic character.

Later constitutional limitations on personal freedoms would extend to Communist ideology. The constitution also required Iran's monarch to adhere to the Ja'afari school of twelver Shi'ism and to defend the faith against external and internal enemies.

In short, the 1906 constitution was not a secular document. Rather, it was an effort to introduce modern systems of government and a measure of governmental accountability in the general framework of Islamic law and morality. But the Pahlavis ignored both these aspects of the constitution. The supervisory role of the religious leaders or 'Ulama', the constitutional provisions on the limitation of the power of the monarch, and the accountability of the executive to a representative assembly were all disregarded. This practice antagonized the Islamic wing of Iranian polity and society and, by alienating the secular intelligentsia, prevented the nurturing of independent secular political institutions in Iran.

Moreover, the personalization of power, its concentration in the monarch, and the distortion of Iranian nationalism into a cult of monarchy undermined nationalist forces and later proved fatal to the whole notion of Iran as the focus of popular allegiance. The Pahlavis made Iranian nationalism the ideological foundation of their rule, using it to legitimize their power and to rationalize their policies. But their notion of nationalism bore little resemblance to Iran's realities, and Iranian nationalism suffered because of its identification with the dynasty.

Instead of seeking the cooperation of reform-minded clerics in the gradual reform of the system, Reza Shah and later his son adopted a confrontational approach toward relations with the clerical establishment. This approach created a deep dichotomy between Islam and nationalism in Iran that greatly contributed to developments culminating in the Islamic revolution of 1979.

By the time of the revolution, Iran's political system bore no resemblance to the one envisaged in the 1906 constitution. All power was concentrated in the person of the shah, the parliament was powerless, and no independent political parties existed. Indeed, Iran had come to resemble a one-party dictatorship because only one party – the officially sanctioned Rastakhiz – was allowed to operate. The perimeters of political debate were also narrowly defined. Only those who were "loyal to the constitution, monarchy, and revolution," the shah's so-called White Revolution, were allowed to participate. Consequently, all opposition groups – religious and secular – were forced underground, and some were engaged in clandestine armed action against the central government.[3]

The lack of open political debate and the inability to bring about change through normal political channels had also led to the formation of an alliance of convenience – along the lines of an informal United Front – among all opposition forces. In addition to disregarding the 1906 constitution's provisions for the conduct of Iran's political life, the Pahlavis' cultural policy had further eroded the political compromise upon which the constitution was based, thereby undermining Iran's national unity. To understand this process, one must first understand the nature of Iran's cultural identity.

Iran's Cultural Identity

Among Muslim countries, Iran is unique in the sense that its pre-Islamic culture has remained extremely strong and relevant to the Iranians' self-identity and to the conduct of their everyday lives. More important, "Iranian Islam" has been deeply influenced by Iran's pre-Islamic philosophical, religious, and cultural traditions.[4]

The intermingling of Iranian culture and Islam has

been so intimate that many recognize a mutual dependence between Iranian nationalism and the Iranian version of Shi'a Islam.[5] Politically, this mutual dependence of Iranian culture and Shi'a Islam was reflected in the modus vivendi that had developed between the king and the Shi'a 'Ulama' during the Safavid period (1502–1736).

The essence of this understanding was that the king enjoyed conditional legitimacy as the defender of Islam and the guarantor of the rule of the Shi'a law in the land. This was a logical partnership because, with the spread of Shi'ism in Iran, Iran's territorial confines had in the eyes of the Shi'as also become the true realm of Islam.

The Shi'a clergy needed the king to protect them and Shi'ism against external enemies, mainly the Sunni Ottomans. The king needed the clergy to legitimize his power. For 400 years, this understanding served Iran well as the country experienced a political and cultural renaissance under the Safavids.

This harmony between Iran and Islam ended, however, when Iran came into contact with the West at the beginning of the nineteenth century. For the Iranians, these first contacts were traumatic and undermined their confidence in their own society and culture.

Iran's defeat by czarist Russia during the two rounds of Russo-Iranian wars (1804–1808 and 1814–1828), the loss of the Transcaucasian provinces, and the imposition of the regime of capitulation, followed by British encroachments in the Persian Gulf and on Iran's eastern front, forced the Iranians to acknowledge a new, profound, and irreversible shift in the balance of forces between Iran and its actual and potential enemies. Until this period, although often conquered by foreigners, Iran had always managed to recover and experience periods of political and cultural renaissance.[6] But the West's scientific and industrial revolution, with far-reaching implications for its military prowess, created such a gap between the West and Iran that it crushed any hope of speedy recovery.

This phenomenon also generated in Iran a deep soul-searching as to why Iran lagged in scientific and industrial advancement. Many Iranians, along with other Muslims, saw religious dogmatism and the contamination of their indigenous Persian culture by foreign Arab and Turkic elements as the principal culprits. Their remedy was secularization, the emulation of Western ways, and cultural purification. In Iran, this meant a greater interest in the country's pre-Islamic past, efforts to rid the Persian language of foreign — especially Arabic — words, and in general, the rise of cultural and political nationalism.[7] Parallel with this development, in the mid-nineteenth century the government made some timid efforts at educational and political reform along these lines.[8]

It is important to note, however, that not everyone agreed with this interpretation of the causes of Iran's — and the Muslims' — decline. Some saw a disregard for Islamic principles and teachings as the primary reason. Their remedy was to apply these principles more strictly. This group certainly did not approve of secularization or any measure that could undermine Islam's central role in defining Iran's cultural and political identity.[9]

These two diverse intellectual trends in Iran's national debate of the late nineteenth century were reflected in its constitutional movement. Thus the secular proponents demanded a constitutional government (Hokoumat-e-Mashruteh) and the Islamic tendency asked for a government by the Shari'a (Hokoumat-e-Mashrueh). Neither, however, could score a clear victory, and the result was the compromise of 1906. Initially in the Iranian political scene, however, the nationalist movement gained the upper hand. Cultural and political nationalism in its novel form became the foundation of Iran's new political institutions and the principal legitimizing and rationalizing concept for the state and its policies.

Several factors related to Iran's internal dynamics and regional and international environment account for this historic victory of nationalism over Islam. First, Iran's new intellectuals were deeply influenced by European ideas of

liberal nationalism and even socialism.[10] Second, many Iranians associated the traditional cultural setting of which
Islam was such an important part with decline. Thus, there
was a sense that for this decline to be reversed, the country
must experience a cultural renaissance. Third, many Iranians of the twentieth century viewed a significant part of
the clerical establishment — rightly or wrongly — as part of a
corrupt elite responsible for Iran's sorry state.

At the regional level, the new Turkish and Arab nation-
alisms that emphasized secularization and modernization were becoming the most powerful ideology. Internationally, during the nineteenth century and for most of the
twentieth century, nationalism was the most powerful political force.

Ironically, disenchantment with secularization and
modernization would undermine nationalism and would
lead to the political and cultural reassertion of Islam in Iran
and throughout the Muslim world. In Iran, as noted, the
Pahlavis' distortion and abuse of nationalism and their arbitrary rule would play the most important role in the cultural
and political reemergence of Islam.

Admittedly, there were extenuating circumstances for
some of the Pahlavis' practices. These included the necessity of creating order in the chaotic Iran of post–World War I,
the unduly extensive presence of foreigners in Iran's social
and political system, and the manipulation of Iran's problems by covetous neighbors and other foreign powers. Nevertheless, the lack of a democratic process and open debate
prevented the maturing of a broad-based notion of Iranian
nationalism. Secular social and political institutions did not
develop, leaving such traditional institutions as the mosque
and bazaar as the only cohesive, albeit often informal, institutional infrastructure.

Furthermore, the Pahlavis went to unreasonable
lengths in their efforts to resurrect a pre-Islamic foundation
for Iranian nationalism and for Iran's collective self-identity. They ignored the tremendous hold of Shi'a Islam on the
Iranians' psyche and the vast contribution of Islam to

Iran's cultural reinvigoration after the third century of its Islamization. Indeed, most of Iran's significant literary, scientific, and philosophical works were written after the country's Islamization. This excess was misguided in two respects: first, the idea of pure "Persianness" that the Pahlavis tried to promote was alien to the majority of — if not all — Iranians and, moreover, was offensive to their religious sensibilities. Most Iranians — including prominent clerics — had long been proud of Iran's past, but the claim that pre-Islamic values were superior to Islam was unacceptable to most Iranians, regardless of its merit.[11]

Second, for the first time since Iran's Islamization — and especially Shi'aization — the Pahlavi policies forced the Iranians to choose between Iran and Islam. Most Iranians resented having to make such a choice, or pushed to the extreme, they chose Islam. The Pahlavis, by portraying this new nationalism based on this unfamiliar and unorthodox view of "Persianness" as a substitute for Islam, turned many Iranians against it.

Third, the Pahlavis turned Iranian nationalism from a notion of loyalty to Iran and its culture into a cult of monarchy — loyalty to the Pahlavis in particular. Nothing illustrates the Pahlavi view of Iranian nationalism better than their slogan of "Khoda, Shah, Mihan" (God, King, Country) where king comes before country. This approach is an important reason why the majority of Iran's nationalists turned away from the Pahlavis and later threw in their lot with Islamic forces.

The Pahlavis also used this interpretation of Iranian nationalism to undermine the clerical establishment and other traditional segments of society. Clearly, by the time the first Pahlavi king came to power, Iran desperately needed reform, including a reduction in the influence of traditional sectors of society. But the way these reforms were implemented left much to be desired. A more gradual and less arbitrary approach, based on a broad social and political consensus and within the confines of constitutional provisions, might have proven more lasting.

This comment particularly applies to the relationship between the government and the clerical establishment. If the Pahlavis had tried to convince the clerics of the necessity of reform and had carried out the reforms in a fair and equitable manner, they might have gained the endorsement of at least more enlightened 'Ulama'.[12] Yet this was not to be the case. On the contrary, the reforms did not benefit large-enough segments of the society, and they were carried out arbitrarily and inequitably. As a result, both the clerical establishment and a significant segment of the Iranian people became alienated from the Pahlavis, their policies, and their ideology – nationalism. This situation led to a strong antinationalist backlash, largely directed by the clerical establishment, and culminated in the Islamic revolution of 1979.

Developments after the Revolution

Iran's revolution of 1979 resulted from the convergence of internal and external factors. Domestically, the cooperation between the regime's religious and secular opponents was very important. Their only common trait, however, was their opposition to the Pahlavi regime. Their views on the shape of Iran's future political system, its cultural basis, and its legitimizing principles diverged sharply.

Three principal ideological trends, each with subcategories, dominated the opposition's views: (1) leftist tendencies covering a wide spectrum from the traditional Communist Tudeh Party to the Islamic-Marxist Mujaheddin-e-Khalq; (2) nationalist groups ranging from traditional liberal nationalists of the Mossadegh tradition to Social Democrats and what could be characterized as Islamic nationalists such as the Freedom Movement of Mehdi Bazargan; and (3) Islamic groups with their stronghold within the clerical establishment, religious schools, the mosques, the bazaar, and a variety of religiously sponsored social and educational organizations. Within the religious groups, the principal division was between the more traditionalist, free market-oriented, and generally more moderate elements and the more radical, socialistically inclined groups.

For the first two years following the fall of the Pahlavi regime, Iran's political scene was dominated by rivalries and jockeying for power among these diverse groups. For a variety of reasons whose discussion is beyond the scope of this study – notably, divisions within the secular groups and rivalry among their leaders – the Islamic tendency prevailed. The first indication of this development appeared when the Iranian people in March 1979 were offered the very narrow choice of voting for or against an Islamic republic and they chose the latter.

Iran's Islamic Constitution and Its Cultural and Ideological Basis

The preamble to Iran's Islamic constitution states that "the basic characteristic of the [Islamic] Revolution, which distinguishes it from other movements that have taken place in Iran during the past hundred years, is its ideological and Islamic nature." The preamble also states that the constitution is the culmination of a century-old Iranian "anti-despotic" and "anti-imperialist" struggle and that the Iranians recognized the failure of previous movements such as the constitutional revolution and Dr. Mohammad Mossadegh's movement to be the lack of a proper ideological and Islamic foundation. Moreover, the preamble states that "the mission of the constitution is to give objective existence to the credal bases of the [Islamic] movement and to create conditions under which may be nurtured the noble and universal values of Islam."

These assertions hold important consequences for the nature of Iran's leadership, its political institutions, and the cultural foundation of its society. First, the basis of political legitimacy and authority in the new constitution is "God" and the divine law as given in the Holy Qur'an, rather than the will of the nation. This approach contrasted with the 1906 constitution, although the "will of the nation" was the source of legitimacy and authority within the limits set by Islamic law and morality. The difference between the two constitutions is not as wide as it may first appear, however, because if the 1906 constitution's provisions had been applied faithfully, no legislation contrary to Islamic law could have passed even if the overwhelming majority of Iranians had approved of it.

Second, because Islam is to be the sole point of reference for all aspects of life, the people running the country must be well versed in Islamic law and be morally irreproachable. This principle is stated in the following way in the preamble of the 1979 Islamic constitution: "The righteous will assume the responsibility of governing and administering the country in accordance with the Qur'anic verse 'Verily my righteous bondsmen inherit the earth.'" The preamble then specifies that "the exercise of meticulous and painstaking supervision by just, pious and committed scholars of Islam (just Fuqaha) is an absolute necessity." Within this framework, the function of ultimate spiritual and political leadership will be discharged by the supreme religious leader on the basis of the concept of the Velayat-e-Faqih or the guardianship of the supreme religious leader. It is this aspect of the 1979 constitution that in effect establishes a system very close to a theocracy. This is unprecedented in Iran's history and certainly goes beyond the supervisory role that the 1906 constitution perceived for the 'Ulama'. In many regards, it is also an innovation in the Shi'a theory of government and political legitimacy.

According to the Shi'a theory, there has not been a legitimate government in the Muslim world since the usurpation of the caliphate from Imam Ali and his descendants. Nor can there be such a government until the return of the twelfth Imam (Messiah). Thus, any government is illegitimate, and the Shi'as owe no allegiance to it.

In practice, however, the Shi'a establishment in Iran accorded conditional legitimacy to the king and the secular government as long as they worked in accordance with Islamic law and respected the position and privileges of the Shi'a clergy. In this theoretical framework, an Islamic government run by the clergy is a complete innovation. Indeed, initially, the Ayatollah Khomeini himself was not against the monarchy as a political system; rather, he opposed what he believed to be the Pahlavis' anti-Islamic policies. He began to develop his concept of an Islamic theocracy after he became convinced that the Pahlavis were beyond redemption and that their rule mortally endangered Islam and the Shi'a establishment in Iran.[13]

Third, in the new Islamic polity, Islam and Islamic notions of nation, state, race, and ethnicity, prevail. In particular, secular nationalism based on ethnic and cultural pride or racial superiority are targeted for elimination. Indeed, soon after gaining power, the Islamic regime dropped any reference to an Iranian nation; its principal point of reference became the Umat-al-Islam (the community of Muslims).

The new government also engaged in a systematic onslaught against nationalist tendencies, "Meli Garai," both in its political and cultural dimensions. In particular, it tried to eradicate any vestiges of Iran's pre-Islamic culture. The new government tried to ban the celebration of Iran's pre-Islamic new year, "Now Rouz." The Ayatollah Khomeini expressed the hope that in the future only the Prophet Mohammad's birthday would be celebrated in Iran. The government also tried to change the Iranian names of the months corresponding to those of Zoroastrian angels and attacked such Persian literary figures as Omar Khayyam and Abol-Ghassem Firdowsi, the author of the Persian nationalist epic *Shahnameh*. Many of Iran's pre-Islamic historic monuments were also damaged. This antinationalist campaign was carried to such unreasonable lengths that even the use of Persian first names was banned.

Unreasonable and destructive as this policy was, it made some political and historical sense. The Islamists, like the nationalists, were aware that culture is not politically neutral and that it has implications for who wields power and who enjoys legitimacy in a society. Moreover, the new regime's antinationalist crusade was a clear retaliation for what they perceived to have been the Pahlavis' anti-Islamic campaign.

Just as Reza Shah and, later, his son used nationalism to bolster their own power, legitimize their position, and undermine the economic and political power base of the clerical establishment, the Islamists used Islam to legitimize their own control of the Iranian polity, delegitimize other forces, and protect their material interests. The Islamists were as mistaken in understanding the true nature of the Iranians' national identity as were the Pahlavis. They underestimated the strength of the Iranians' attachment to the "Iranian" component of their culture—the extent to which Persian culture had permeated and molded what could be fairly characterized as "Iranian Islam"—as much as the Pahlavis had underestimated the strength of Shi'a Islam's hold on Iran.

Popular reaction to the government's antinationalist policy was negative and strong. External events such as the Iraqi invasion of Iran in September of 1980 strengthened nationalist sentiments. The Islamic government had to relent on its antinationalist campaign. It even had to resort to Iranian nationalism to mobilize resistance against Iraq. The Islamic/nationalist dichotomy has not ended in Iran. But in the past few years, these two poles of the Iranian culture have gradually moved toward reconciliation. The rehabilitation of Iranian nationalism, however, has not reached such a level as to be granted equal weight with Islam. Thus, its influence has not filtered into Iran's political institutions. But if this process continues, nationalism's influence will be reflected in Iran's political institutions and in their legal foundations.

Contradictions in the 1979 Constitution and Its Reform

The political system set up in Iran following the Islamic revolution and embodied in the constitution of 1979 had built-in contradictions and inconsistencies. During the past decade, these characteristics caused governmental indecision and inefficiency, incurring heavy losses for the country. The Iranian leadership has been aware of these problems.

Even during the Ayatollah Khomeini's lifetime, periodic efforts were made to resolve these contradictions.

In the summer of 1989, the constitution was finally amended, resolving some of the problems, especially those related to the structure of executive and judicial powers. Moreover, the qualities required for the supreme religious leader were reinterpreted to expedite the transition of power. Some fundamental issues, however, regarding the qualifications of the supreme religious leader, the process of choosing him, the mechanism for resolving differences between the parliament and the Guardian Council over legislation and its compatibility with Islamic law, the role of political parties, and so on remain either unresolved or ambiguous. How the debate on these issues evolves and how these contradictions are or are not resolved will to a great extent determine the fate of the Islamic regime and the shape of Iran's political system and institutions.

The outcome of this debate will also determine whether political change in Iran will be peaceful and evolutionary or violent and sudden. Before discussing the 1989 constitutional amendments and how they may affect politics and policy in Iran, the principal sources of contradiction and inconsistency in Iran's 1979 constitution must be noted. These fall into two categories: (1) those related to the nature of the Shi'a political theory, the nature of Islamic law and jurisprudence, and the process of leadership formation within the Shi'a clerical establishment; and (2) the division of the executive power between the president and the prime minister, lack of clarity regarding their respective power, and the absence of a mechanism to deal with the stalemate that can, and often did, arise between the president and the prime minister.

Velayat-e-Faqih, Islamic Law, and
the Shi'a Theory of Government

The centerpiece of Iran's Islamic legal and political system is the institution of the guardianship of the supreme religious leader. As noted earlier, this guardianship is an innovation in the Shi'a theory of government and political legitimacy.

The Velayat-e-Faqih is not the same as the "Islamic supervision" provided for in the 1906 constitution, which imparts limited legitimacy to government run by nonreligious bureaucrats. Rather, according to the 1979 constitution, the Velayat-e-Faqih would lead to the creation of a truly Islamic government that, by definition, must be just and legitimate and hence against traditional Shi'a theory, under which such a government would be achieved only by the return of the twelfth Imam. It is precisely because of this theoretical inconsistency that many prominent religious figures in Iran opposed the establishment of the Velayat-e-Faqih, although they supported the supremacy of Islamic law, the supervisory role of the 'Ulama', and the general Islamization of Iran.

In addition to its theoretically innovative character, the rule of the Velayat-e-Faqih entails problems deriving from the informal character of the traditional mode of selecting Shi'a religious leaders who are sources of emulation (Marja-e-Taglid), plus the requirement of the 1979 constitution that the supreme religious leader be a source of emulation. In the past, an incremental consensus within the clerical establishment determined who were the two or three most learned and respected religious leaders with the largest following. Thus no individual or council can determine the sources of emulation from whose ranks the supreme religious leader should be chosen. Religious leaders are recognized as Marja-e-Taglid, or they are not.

The fact is that the Velayat-e-Faqih was instituted to provide a constitutional basis for the Ayatollah Khomeini's leadership. Yet the Ayatollah Khomeini's undisputed claims to leadership derived not from his religious qualities as a source of emulation, although he possessed these qualities, but from his political role as the leader of the revolution.

Because the Ayatollah Khomeini met both the religious and political criteria for supreme religious leader, the difficulties involved in reconciling these different requirements after he passed from the scene were not apparent during the first years of the revolution. But by 1985, as the Ayatollah Khomeini's health began to fade, the issue of his successor as the next supreme religious leader became a matter of urgency. The debate that this situation generated and the way it was finally resolved showed the political rather than religious nature of Velayat-e-Faqih and the lack of its firm foundation in traditional Shi'a theory.

The Ayatollah Hossein Ali Montazeri was selected as the next supreme religious leader and the successor to Ayatollah Khomeini on political grounds. He was later dismissed from that position on the same grounds. Indeed, on the basis of how Shi'a leaders are traditionally selected, he would hardly have emerged as among the two or three most learned and respected leaders. Indeed, he himself often said that he was not a Marja-e-Taglid and that he emulated the Ayatollah Khomeini. Montazeri's claim to leadership derived from his role in the opposition to the shah and his contribution to the Islamic revolution. The loss of his claim was political, too: he fell out with the Ayatollah Khomeini and his close associates. Similarly, the selection of Hodjat-al-Islam Khamenei as the new faqih was a political act; it was the result of uneasily won consensus among major political players. In fact, in this respect, the leaders of Islamic Iran resemble other revolutionary leaders whose legitimacy derives from their revolutionary struggle more than any other source.

In short, the lack of a solid theological foundation for Velayat-e-Faqih in Shi'ism and the lack of a clear process for selecting religious leaders qualified to assume the mantle of supreme leader will continue to pose constitutional difficulties for the Islamic regime. This problem could become acute after the generation of leaders who derive their legitimacy from their role in the Islamic revolution and their associations with Ayatollah Khomeini leave the scene. Indeed, how this problem is resolved – or not resolved, as the case may be – will determine the shape of Iran's political system.

What Kind of Islamic Law?

Another fundamental constitutional problem derives from
the very nature of Islamic law; thus, it is unlikely to be
easily resolved. In the Islamic republic, the source of law is
the will of God as expressed in the Qur'an. According to the
Ayatollah Khomeini, the parliament of an Islamic government cannot legislate. All it can do is to set "programs of
action" (Barnameh-Ghozari) based on the Islamic law.

Yet, in regard to many important issues in economic
and social policy such as land reform and the role of the
private sector, Islam has no clear laws. Even Qur'anic verses and sayings attributed to the prophet of Islam and other
Muslim notables in relation to these issues are subject to
different interpretations. Indeed, over the centuries, varying interpretations by Muslim jurists have added to legal
ambiguities and contradictions by developing different legal schools and different opinions within each school.

This basic problem has given rise to the difficulties
faced by the Iranian regime as it tries to develop clear and
sustained policies. In the past, an issue of this nature was
resolved by a decree of the Ayatollah Khomeini, not through
consensus among Islamic jurists or by a parliamentary majority. In this sense, Ayatollah Khomeini was the source of
law – a situation not encouraging for the maturing of Iran's
political system and the strengthening of its institutions
and legal systems. The constitutional reforms of 1989 have
not resolved this basic problem. Thus, the regime will not
easily resolve the legal controversy over economic, social,
and political issues. Resolution will be particularly difficult
in reconciling the requirements of economic development
and social justice and equity, because different groups will
justify their positions on the basis of some Qur'anic verse or
some saying of the Prophet or Imam Ali. The resolution of
these dilemmas will depend on the evolution of the balance
of power within the leadership. In other words, in all likelihood, one interpretation representing the preferences and
interests of certain segments will be given precedence over

another interpretation, even if the latter view represents the majority view. But this situation will alienate other groups, prevent the development of a reasonably broad-based consensus, and thus further delay the maturing of Iran's political institutions.

The situation does not need to be as grim, however, as the foregoing implies. With enlightened and fair-minded leadership and the judicious use of existing instruments and institutions (or the establishment of new ones), these difficulties could be mitigated, if not totally overcome. By judiciously exercising "Ijtihad" (interpretation of Islamic principles by the 'Ulama'), for example, progressive and reform-minded 'Ulama' can adapt Islamic principles to the requirements of the modern world. The Guardian Council (the body responsible for ensuring the compatibility of any legislation with Islamic law and for interpreting the articles of the Constitution) could perform a task similar to that of the Supreme Court in the United States, sorting legal opinions and arriving at interpretations that then acquire legal force. In the process, they could develop a modern, coherent, flexible, and tolerant body of Islamic law and jurisprudence.

On several occasions in his Friday prayer sermons, President Rafsanjani has indicated the important role an enlightened Ijtihad can play. The Ayatollah Khomeini himself on two occasions used his power of Ijtihad by interpreting rules regarding chess and music in Islam. He declared that chess was not gambling and that music was acceptable if not used for un-Islamic and corrupt purposes.

The parliament could be made into a more effective and representative body that could decide on delicate issues within Islam's moral and spiritual limits and in accordance with economic efficiency and social justice. But this would only happen if political parties were allowed to form and the base of participants in the electoral process was enlarged. After the dissolution of the Islamic Republican Party – the principal power base of Islamic groups after the revolution – Iran has no real political parties; only certain political associations consisting mostly of clerical political groups, including the following, are allowed to function:

1. The Resalat Foundation, which has its origin in the Theology Teachers' Association. It publishes the daily *Resalat*. It believes in traditional Islamic jurisprudence and is against government intervention in the economy.
2. The Tehran Militant Clergy Association, which was formed in 1978. Its membership includes most of the leadership of the Islamic movement, including Iran's current president, Ayatollah Rafsanjani.
3. Tehran Militant Clerics, formed in 1988 when the more radical figures left the TMCA.

Needless to say, these groups do not represent the whole spectrum of Iranian politics, which makes it difficult to reach a more broad-based political consensus and to overlook fringe elements. By 1991 there was some indication that the government might allow the formation of other parties that do not challenge the basic legitimacy of the regime. If Iran can succeed in this endeavor, it would render a great service to Islam by ushering in a true age of Islamic reform and by creating a progressive and representative Islamic political system. Creating such a system, however, would be a lengthy and difficult process. Currently, any talk of Islamic reform is attacked by the hard-liners as heresy and as liberal subversion against the teachings of Ayatollah Khomeini.

Non-Islamic Difficulties

The division of executive power between the president and the prime minister in the 1979 constitution also created serious obstacles to effective governance. According to Article 113 of the 1979 constitution, the president was not a mere ceremonial figurehead, but "the highest official position in the country" after the supreme leader. He was responsible for implementing the constitution, ordering relations among the three powers, and heading the executive power except in matters pertaining directly to the leadership. He nominated the prime minister and could accept or reject the ministers chosen by the prime minister, thus also influencing policy, although according to Article 134 the prime minister was primarily responsible for determining "the program and policies of the government."

As long as the views of the president and the prime minister are in perfect harmony, such a system can work. But given the fractious nature of Iran's leadership, this situation — together with other problems such as disagreements between the parliament and the Guardian Council — nearly paralyzed the government for several years.

Debate on Constitutional Reform and Its Outcome

Iran's constitutional debate officially started on April 24, 1989. Just a few weeks before his death, in a letter to Iran's then-President Hodjat-al-Islam Ali Khamenei, the Ayatollah Khomeini recognized the necessity of constitutional reform and appointed a 20-member body to study the constitution and to propose necessary amendments within two months.[14] In his letter, he stated that as part of his religious and national duty, he had given this matter some thought but that the war and other issues had prevented him from focusing on it.

The body formed for this purpose was officially called the Council for the Reappraisal of the Constitution of the Islamic Republic of Iran. It had 25 members; 20 of them were directly appointed by Ayatollah Khomeini, and 5 were chosen by the parliament. Of the members, 17 had served in various capacities in the legislative and executive bodies, and 14 were members of the Assembly of Experts that had approved the 1979 constitution.[15]

The council was to deal with three principal issues: the

qualifications of leadership—that is, the question of the Ayatollah Khomeini's successor, the question of the division of executive power, and the composition of the judiciary. Other, relatively minor issues were also to be reviewed and amended:

- Management of the Voice and Vision (Iranian radio and television) in such a way that the three branches would have supervision over it;
- Reassessment of the number of parliament deputies;
- The working of the Council of Discerning What Is Good in order to solve the problems of the regime and enable it to consult with the leadership in a way that would not present it as a power competing with other branches;
- A way to review the constitution;
- Changing the name of the National Consultative Assembly to *Islamic* Consultative Assembly.

The amendments agreed upon by the council would then be put to a public referendum. As might be expected, the thorniest issue, and the one with the greatest potential consequence, concerned the qualifications of the person or persons who alone or collectively were to function as the supreme religious leader.

The 1979 constitution required that the supreme religious leader, in addition to all other qualifications, be a source of emulation, a Marja-e-Taglid. This requirement, however, posed a serious dilemma for the Islamic leadership in identifying an acceptable successor to the Ayatollah Khomeini.

Among the few existing sources of emulation in the Shi'a world, none had the physical strength, personal inclination, or political acceptability to become the supreme religious leader. And those within the leadership, or the Ayatollah's family, who would have met the physical and political criteria were not sources of emulation. This problem was resolved when the council decided that not only the existing sources of emulation, but also those who were qualified to become sources of emulation, could be chosen as supreme leader. Moreover, during the debate, a number of prominent clerical leaders, including the Grand Ayatollah Azeri-Qomi, emphasized that having the qualifications to be a source of emulation alone was not sufficient. Any prospective leader must also have a thorough knowledge of government and society.[16]

By accepting the above criteria, the council separated the functions of leadership (Rahbariat) from being a source of emulation (Marjai'at). This political compromise was intended to open the way for selecting Hodjat-al-Islam Khamenei as the leader because, as noted earlier, there is no clear procedure to ascertain who is, or can be, a source of emulation. Religious leaders either are sources of emulation and are recognized as such by their peers and their followers, or they are not. In reality, therefore, the constitutional amendment stripped the office of the supreme religious leader and the selection process of religious consideration and made it even more of a political office than it was before. Thus, in the future, the supreme religious leader will be chosen not through the incremental unstructured process of emerging sources of emulation, but through the political consensus — or at least compromise — among principal political players that occurs when choosing the leader of a secular political party.

Although this amendment solved the immediate problem of finding a successor to the Ayatollah Khomeini, it did not resolve the long-term problem of choosing the next supreme religious leader, because it did not establish a selection process or come up with a complete list of selection criteria, religious or otherwise. The lack of agreed standards of religious qualifications bedeviled the Islamic government later during the election of members of the Assembly of Experts, which has the power to elect the future supreme leader. During the elections, which were held in the fall of 1990, several key radical clerical figures — even including the Ayatollah Mehdi Karubi, speaker of the Iranian parliament, and the Ayatollah Sadeq Khalkhali – were disqualified from running for election by the Guardian Council, which was responsible for ascertaining their competence in Islamic law, theology, and jurisprudence. These disqualifications reflected the ascendancy of the moderate wing of the Iranian leadership and led to bitter complaints on the part of the radicals. They accused the Khamenei-Rafsanjani leadership of wanting to concentrate all power in their own hands and those of their supporters as a way of undermining the "revolutionary and democratic character" of the Islamic regime.

Although this disqualification was a positive development as far as the evolution of Iran's political scene is concerned, the process itself is unlikely to help develop solid political institutions. And if the fortunes of the radical wing change, the radicals almost certainly will try to exclude the moderates from the existing political institutions.[17]

The immediate result of these developments was open conflict and public recrimination between the moderates and radicals. Some radical figures openly challenged the Ayatollah Khamenei's religious qualifications, highlighting the inherent weaknesses of the theological foundations of the institution of supreme religious leader.[18]

The long-term impact of these changes on the Shi'a establishment's influence and political role in Iran cannot be predicted. Indeed, while consolidating the power of the present clerical leadership, these changes – which are part and parcel of a broader and ongoing subordination of religion to political necessity in Iran – could be the beginning of a drastic reduction in the political influence of that establishment. They might even be the beginning of an Islamic reformation that might more clearly delineate the domains of politics and religion and the roles of religious and political leaders in the society. In fact, during the debate on constitutional reform, some noted that the separation of the leadership from being a source of emulation could mark the beginning of the separation of religion from politics.[19]

Traditionally the Shi'a establishment in Iran has drawn

its influence from the following sources: its independent financial base, its distance from the day-to-day operations of government, and an underlying notion of the illegitimacy, or at best limited legitimacy, of any government. Because of these factors, the Shi'a establishment has exerted tremendous political influence without incurring any responsibility or blame, while maintaining its position as the guardian of religious purity.

Precisely for these reasons, many prominent Shi'a clergy were and still are against the Velayat-e-Faqih and intimate involvement of the clergy in politics. They have preferred a supervisory role along the lines of the 1906 constitution, leaving the day-to-day task of governing to professional classes. But being in charge of running the government, the clergy cannot escape popular blame for its deficiencies. Moreover, government failure undermines popular belief in the religious principles used by the clergy as the basis and justification for its policies, thus weakening the hold of religion in the society and by extension the clergy's influence. In short, the constitutional amendments in this regard have not resolved the long-term problems of governance in Iran. They have not clarified the source of political legitimacy in the country nor have they resolved the inherent tension between religious rules and political necessities. Nevertheless, constitutional reforms and the open debate preceding them have been positive developments on the long road that Iran has to travel toward political and institutional maturation. Iran must develop a political theory that is based on its historical religious and cultural values but yet responds to the requirements of running a modern society.

The Nature of Executive Power

The council's second most important task was to establish a clear center of executive decision making and to define its relationship to the legislature.

The debate on this issue revolved around the following

basic theme: should Iran have a presidential-style executive branch with powers concentrated in a presidency responsible only to the parliament, or should it have a parliamentary-style executive? In the latter case, the presidency would have become a ceremonial position and the prime minister the principal executive official. Those who were against the presidential system feared that the concentration of power in the presidency could lead to dictatorship. These people favored either the continuation of the division of executive power between the president and the prime minister or strict parliamentary supervision over the president. The question of the relationship between the president and the parliament—especially whether the president or the supreme religious leader should be able to dissolve the parliament—was hotly debated.

The constitutional debate occurred simultaneously with preparations for the presidential elections. Consequently, different factions based their attitudes toward a presidential system largely on their expectations for the success of their favorite candidates. The reverse was also true; the different factions supported different candidates according to their expectations of what sort of system—presidential or parliamentary—each candidate would adopt. The hard-liners, for example, initially backed the candidacy of the then-speaker of parliament, Hodjat-al-Islam Hashemi Rafsanjani. They expected that in a parliamentary system, the presidency would become a ceremonial position. By controlling the parliament and having effective control over the choice of the prime minister, they would set the policy.

Some also feared that a strong presidency, especially if the post of prime minister were eliminated, would void the parliament's control over the executive branch. According to an editorial in the *Tehran Times*, "it would no longer allow the Majlis to give its vote of confidence to the president's choice for premiership."[20] This criticism, however, is invalid, because presidential appointments could always be made subject to parliamentary approval. This is indeed what happened. Under the amended constitution, parliamentary supervision of the presidency is even more stringent because the parliament has the right to question the president. If the parliament finds the president's explanations inadequate, it can appeal to the supreme religious leader to dismiss the president in the interests of the country, even though the president is elected by popular vote. If the political base of the electorate is limited, however, and the elections are less than fair, the parliament may not, in practice, be able to offer an effective counterweight to the executive power.

The other controversial issue involving the relative power of the parliament was the suggestion that the supreme religious leader should be allowed to dissolve the parliament under certain circumstances. This suggestion, which was ratified by the Council for the Reappraisal of the Constitution, led to a protest by 177 members of parliament. They argued that the 1979 constitution stipulated that parliament should function under all conditions. More important, they pointed out that Ayatollah Khomeini never intended the role of parliament to be undermined.

The controversy over the respective roles and powers of the president, the supreme religious leader, and the parliament, in addition to legal and philosophical differences on the intrinsic merits of a parliamentary, presidential, or mixed system, reflected intraregime ideological differences about the country's domestic and international direction, as well as personal rivalries for power.

As the outlines of joint leadership by Rafsanjani and Khamenei became apparent, the radicals feared for their own future influence. They tried to enhance the parliament's power—or at least prevent any diluting of its privileges—because there at least for a time they were sure of having considerable presence. In this way, they hoped to exert significant influence over policy and to prevent the moderates from diluting what they saw as the revolution's principles. The system that emerged was a strengthened but not omnipotent presidency whose powers are checked by the prerogatives of the spiritual leader and the parliament. The new arrangements also imply a more collegial system of governance for Iran, one based on building consensus rather than issuing orders. This system is a novelty in Iran's recent history and a step forward compared with the one-man rule of the past. The current system, however, can function effectively only as long as the two principal personalities—the president and the supreme leader— agree. Otherwise it would either break down or degenerate into one-man rule. Although falling far short of resolving the dilemma of orderly transfer of power and effective governance in Iran, these constitutional reforms are thus a step in the right direction. They have enabled the leadership to act more rapidly and forcefully on issues of vital concern to the country. In areas such as foreign policy, however, where there are differences of opinion between the president and the supreme leader, the dual character of leadership has been a handicap. It has delayed the adjustment of Iran's foreign policy to new international conditions.

The Composition of the Judiciary

Another important item in the constitutional debate was the composition of judicial power and the identification of the principal source of authority within this body. The structure and functions of the judiciary in the 1979 constitution are detailed in Articles 156 to 174. The constitution of 1979 had aimed to reverse the secularizing trend of the Pahlavi era. It clearly based the judicial system on Islamic law and stipulated that principal judicial officials should be chosen from among the Mujtahid, the highest level of religious leader expert in Islamic law and jurisprudence.

According to Article 157, the highest judicial power was a council known as the Supreme Judicial Council. The council had five members, including the head of the Supreme Court, the prosecutor-general, and three judges of proven fairness and possessing the quality of Mujtahid, to be chosen by all the judges of the country.

According to the 1979 constitution, the Ministry of Justice was merely an administrative body. The minister of justice was only an administrator serving as liaison between the judiciary, the executive, and legislative branches.

Given the nature of the Islamic law and the diversity of opinion among Islamic scholars, the collective structure of the judiciary was a sure recipe for confusion and inaction. The situation was rendered particularly difficult because the constitution failed to provide a mechanism for resolving differences of opinion among the council members and for reaching decisions. The council was also responsible for managing the judicial system, which further complicated matters. Unlike the debate on the nature and privileges of the executive branch, there was no major divergence of opinion among different groups about the sources of difficulties in the judiciary and their remedies.

It was generally agreed that the collective format of the council had to be changed. That is exactly what was done. The amendment to Article 157 replaced the council with a "just and resourceful Mujtahid well-versed in judiciary affairs," which shall be elected as head of the judicial branch for five years. This made the administration of justice more manageable, but did not remove the problem of resolving differences of opinion on legal matters rooted in the nature of Islamic law.

Developments Following Constitutional Reform

The constitutional amendments were put to popular vote simultaneously with the presidential elections of July 1989 and were duly ratified. These changes eliminated some of the deficiencies of the 1979 constitution and eased the transition to the post-Khomeini era. By eliminating the condition that the future faqih be a source of emulation, for example, the amendments paved the way for the Ayatollah Khamenei's succession. By eliminating the post of prime minister, they removed a significant source of governmental

confusion and inertia. But by making the president responsible to parliament for his ministers' actions and by enabling the parliament to force ministers out by a vote of no
confidence at any time, the amendments limited the president's freedom.

Other amendments should help create a more effective
and rational executive. According to the new Article 131,
for instance, the president can appoint one or more vice
presidents, called assistants.

A Supreme National Security Council (SNSC) is designed to facilitate decision making and to create a forum
where different options can be discussed and a consensus
developed. According to the new Article 176, the SNSC
would

• formulate defense and national security policies
within the bounds of general policies determined by the
leader;
• harmonize state programs in areas relating to politics
and collect intelligence reports, as well as develop social,
cultural, and economic activities in relation to general defense and security policies; and
• exploit Iran's material and intellectual resources for
countering threats against the country.

The president presides over the SNSC. Its membership
consists of the following: The heads of the three branches of
government, the chief of the Supreme Command Council of
the Armed Forces, the official in charge of National Budget
and Planning Affairs, two representatives from the supreme religious leader, the minister of foreign affairs, the
minister of the interior, the minister of information, a cabinet minister as the situation may warrant, and the highest
ranking officials in the armed forces and the Sepah (Islamic
Revolutionary Guards Corps).

Even with these constitutional reforms, Iran's post-
Khomeini government has not been able to act as quickly
and as decisively as the circumstances require on several

key issues. Differences of opinion within the regime have persisted, and the ways of resolving them have not yet been worked out. The principal difficulty in this regard is that these differences do not merely reflect ideological disagreements, but diverging interests of the regime's various constituencies. Thus, the regime cannot move too far in one direction without undermining its own base of support. Certainly, no such move can be made without some effort at consensus building and persuasion. Although this process in itself has merit, its principal shortcoming is that it does not allow the quick and decisive action Iran's problems require. Ultimately the moderate wing of the leadership may find it necessary to develop new partnerships outside the revolutionary leadership that would enable it to overlook the resistance of the hard-liners.

Two factors, however, make such an eventuality problematic, although not impossible. First, to make such a partnership a viable option, the regime would have to make considerable concessions to secular forces amenable to such cooperation, which could dangerously dilute its revolutionary character. Second, without such concessions, the regime may find it very difficult to convince even the most malleable of the opposition groups – such as ex-Prime Minister Mehdi Bazargan's – to join in such a partnership. The radical elements would do all they could to prevent the regime's moderate wing from accommodating with segments of the secular opposition or with apolitical elements mainly concerned about a more tolerant social and political environment and economic prosperity. Indeed, some radicals complain that the regime has not been harsh enough toward those they accuse of "liberal subversion against Islam" and acting as a fifth column for the West. Herein lies the regime's most significant dilemma. To succeed in the economic reconstruction, political consolidation, and international rehabilitation essential for its survival, the regime must liberalize, isolate its radicals, and broaden the base of its support. But by doing so, it would have to dilute, and perhaps abandon, some of its own principal characteristics. It would thus risk losing the support of some of its current partisans and, more ominously, trigger a stronger reaction from the radicals.

The other alternative is for one group to gain a decisive influence over the other faction. This is a more likely outcome and may resolve some of the short-term problems of governance. But in the long term, if the parameters of political debate and the base of its participants are not broadened, the development of solid and generally democratic institutions for orderly transfer of power would be delayed and the future stability of Iran remain in doubt. The victory of one faction outside the framework of general liberalization would lead once more to an overconcentration of power and the personalization of the decision-making apparatus. Large segments of the community would be alienated, a sure recipe for long-term troubles. Should the radicals win the contest, moreover, the country's problems would be exacerbated, and the limited advances in Iran's rehabilitation and integration into the international community would be reversed.

Thus far, however, the regime has not been able to take bold action to broaden its base of support. Nor, despite the moderates' gains, has one group gained a decisive victory over the other. Nearly three years after the Ayatollah Khomeini's death, the conduct of Iran's policy is still marred by the regime's internal contradictions.

The Persian Gulf War once more highlighted intraregime differences. Moderate, pragmatic elements led by President Rafsanjani promoted a cautious and balanced policy based on two principles: (1) condemnation of Iraq's invasion of Kuwait and support for the UN call for Iraqi withdrawal from Kuwait and UN-imposed economic sanctions; and (2) opposition to the long-term presence of foreign, especially U.S., forces in the region.

The radicals, led by such people as Hodjat-al-Islam Mohtashami and Ayatollah Sadeq Khalkhali, argued that Iran should forget its past conflict with Iraq and join hands with them in opposing their common enemy—the United States.

The moderates prevailed in this debate, to a great ex-

tent because the radicals' views did not have much reso-
nance among the Iranian people. Yet controversy over
Iran's position toward Iraq, its attitude toward the presence
of foreign forces in the region, and the future of Persian
Gulf security continued to bedevil the leadership even after
Gulf hostilities ceased.

When popular revolts broke out in Iraq, including in the
heavily Shi'a-populated areas of southern Iraq, the radicals
once more urged active Iranian support for Iraq's Shi'as.
The moderate pragmatists, realizing that any direct and
large-scale Iranian interference in Iraq could trigger a conflict with U.S. forces stationed in southern Iraq, resisted
such pressures. But the ruthless suppression of the Shi'a
uprising by Saddam Hussein's remaining military forces
and the massive damage done to Shi'a holy shrines, while
Iran remained on the sidelines, gave new ammunition to the
radicals for attacking the moderates' policies. Yet the moderates' ability to prevail during the sensitive period of the
Persian Gulf War and in its turbulent aftermath indicate
that the trend toward greater moderation of Iranian politics
has become stronger and more popular domestically. The
radicals will still continue to exploit any opportunity to
undermine the moderates and their realistic policies.

With these intraregime divisions still casting a shadow
over Iran's future, the danger of a return to the hard-line
and destructive policies of the past, though reduced, has
not been completely removed. Such ideological differences
will continue to affect post-Khomeini politics in Iran.

The Moderate-Radical Dichotomy:
An Accurate Term?

Since at least 1984, differences of opinion within the Iranian leadership have been explained in light of a moderate-
radical paradigm. This split came to the fore during the
Iran-contra debacle of 1985–1986. Amid the Iran-contra
controversy, most Western, especially U.S., analysts of Iranian affairs dismissed the idea of any significant differences

of opinion within the Iranian leadership. Yet such a dismissal was more the result of their frustration over the failure of U.S. policy than a reflection of Iran's political realities.

Differences of opinion have always existed within Iran's Islamic movement and its leadership. This philosophical difference was enhanced as various elements within the leadership reacted differently to the experience of governing and dealing with the outside world. But the split within the leadership has never been as stark as the moderate-radical paradigm implies. There have always been shades of moderation and radicalism. At times, some political leaders have held radical views on certain issues but more moderate views on others.[21] Moreover, some figures who started out as radicals have become more pragmatic and less ideological, if not exactly moderate by conviction. Nevertheless, in its essentials, the moderate-radical paradigm explains the principal division within Iran's leadership.

In broad terms, the moderates have a more traditional interpretation of Islam. They favor a free enterprise economic system, stressing Islam's sanctioning of private property. Thus, they oppose massive land reform and other policies akin to socialist and statist systems. Although committed to maintaining Iran's Islamic character, they interpret Islamic moral codes more flexibly and hence are more lenient in enforcing them.

In foreign affairs, the moderates have tended to be strongly anti-Soviet, favoring a balanced approach toward relations with both Eastern and Western bloc countries. But since 1987, this aspect of intraregime differences has lost its significance, owing largely to changes in the Soviet Union and in the Soviet approach to Iran and to the subsequent warming of Soviet-Iranian relations. In general, the moderates have opposed a provocative and belligerent international posture. They have favored better ties with the West, including, under certain circumstances, the United States.

The moderates have also been more willing to learn from past mistakes. Being more pragmatic, they have been more ready to adapt to new realities. Nationalist tendencies — nationalist in the sense that they tend to give priority to Iran's national and state interests rather than vague ideological aspirations — are stronger among the moderates. The moderates' principal constituency is within the business community, middle classes, and the bureaucracy.

The radicals, by contrast, have a more revolutionary interpretation of Islam, emphasizing its egalitarian dimensions and its admonitions against the undue accumulation of wealth. In principle, they favor a centralized and statist economy, massive land reforms, and even large-scale government control of foreign trade. Because their policies have failed so resoundingly, however, they have moderated their views in the past few years, now accepting a greater role for private enterprise. The collapse of socialist systems and the global trend toward privatization have further weakened the radicals' economic arguments.

The radicals champion a strict application of the Islamic moral code. Their attitude is determined more by political and cultural concerns, however, than by religious piety. They fear, for example, that any relaxation of Islamic morality would allow what they see as decadence in Western culture, as well as in traditional Persian culture, to creep back in and dilute Iran's revolutionary character.

They also fear that any improvement in social atmosphere in Iran might encourage the exiles to return. They fiercely oppose such a return because they believe that, too, would lead to the revolution's dilution. But even more important, the private fortunes of some radicals engaged in the Revolutionary Guards and a variety of Islamic committees have been involved in this debate. With a more flexible interpretation of these rules and a more relaxed social atmosphere, the raison d'être of these elements would disappear.

In foreign affairs, the radicals are fiercely opposed to the United States. Nor do they favor extensive ties with other Western countries. Pro-Soviet sentiments have been strong among elements of the radicals, prompting Foreign

Minister Ali-Akbar Velayati at one time to call them "left-ists with an Islamic veneer."[22] In the past, most radicals favored aggressive exporting of the revolution, including the use of subversion.

In the last few years the more technocratic radicals have come to realize the disastrous consequences of this approach for Iran. The radicals' constituency is among the lower classes, the younger generation of clerical students, elements of the bureaucracy, and the Revolutionary Guards. The principal appeal of the radicals is their portrayal of themselves as the champions of Islamic purity and of the rights of the deprived.

Until 1988, the two factions were more or less equal in strength within the leadership and in their base of support among the supporters of the Islamic regime. Although there were periodic shifts in the relative influence of these two factions, these shifts were never decisive or long-lasting, partly because the Ayatollah Khomeini was unwilling to endorse one group unequivocally.

By the time the Ayatollah Khomeini died, however, the disastrous consequences of the radicals' policies on Iran's domestic conditions and regional and international position had largely discredited the radicals' vision and undermined their influence among the public. Indeed, the degradation of Iran's situation had become so severe that continuing the radicals' line could very well have meant political suicide for the regime. The death of the Ayatollah Khomeini also weakened the radicals' position because they could no longer seek his assistance in maintaining and restoring a balance between the two factions.

The Rafsanjani Presidency and the Moderate-Radical Dichotomy

The Ayatollah Rafsanjani's election to Iran's presidency was seen as a victory for the moderate faction. This perception was only partially justified, as the record of his presidency indicates. The first factor limiting the power of Rafsanjani, and hence of the moderates, has been the nature of the political system that emerged after the constitutional reforms.

As noted, while the presidency was strengthened, the parliament retained considerable power over policy. Because the radicals still have considerable influence within the parliament, this situation limits Rafsanjani's freedom of action. Indeed, after finally approving the cabinet presented by President Rafsanjani on August 29, 1989, the speaker of the Iranian parliament, the relatively radical Ayatollah Mehdi Karubi, warned that the parliament should not be considered a mere rubber stamp.

Second, even some of Rafsanjani's closest allies, including the new faqih, the Ayatollah Khamenei, did not want to see him emerge as Iran's uncontested leader. Thus, only two months after his appointment as the commander in chief of the armed forces, Rafsanjani relinquished his position, saying he needed to devote all his time to the country's economic recovery. The post of commander in chief was assumed by the Ayatollah Khamenei. Although President Rafsanjani certainly has his hands full with Iran's economic problems, his relinquishing control of the military diluted his power.

The new spiritual leader can be characterized as moderate by necessity and, in some regards, particularly in foreign policy, much more hard-line than President Rafsanjani. Hence, he has often acted to check the moderates from moving too fast in redirecting Iran's foreign policy, especially as regards any improvement in ties with the United States. This difference became clear once more during the Persian Gulf crisis; while the Ayatollah Khamenei reacted harshly to the U.S. presence in the Persian Gulf, President Rafsanjani adopted a more low-key approach.

Third, although the radical faction's position has been weakened, the faction maintains a core of supporters that can create serious difficulties for the new leadership. Immediately after the Ayatollah Khomeini's death, the political ambitions of his son Ahmad were unclear. For a while, the radicals hoped he might be persuaded to run for the presidency—hopes that were disappointed as Hojdat-al-Islam Khomeini gave his support to the emerging leadership of Khamenei-Rafsanjani.

Despite these limitations, President Rafsanjani has tried to steer Iran's politics in a moderate direction. The cabinet he presented to parliament on August 19, 1989, was heavily weighted in favor of those who could best be described as "pragmatic technocrats," with eight of his top ministers being the graduates of either U.S. or European universities.[23]

Parliamentary debate on the proposed cabinet was lively, with some delegates criticizing the educational background of some of the ministers before the cabinet was finally endorsed.[24] President Rafsanjani has also tried to neutralize some of the radical figures by appointing them to advisory positions and to the National Security Council.

Initially, this need to placate the radicals inhibited the Rafsanjani administration from making the needed reforms quickly. Rafsanjani's gradual and cautious approach, however, prevented an early polarization of the political scene and total alienation of the radicals. In the summer of 1990, external developments enhanced the moderates' position, and there were moves toward further isolating prominent radical figures. Nevertheless, the contest is not over.

A critical test of the relative fortunes of the two factions may be the parliamentary elections to be held in the spring of 1992. The hope is that the moderates will win a clear majority, thus freeing President Rafsanjani to pursue his reforms more vigorously. But the radicals will try to exploit hardships caused by Rafsanjani's necessary economic reforms and use public satisfaction to their own advantage.

The Need for Professionalism
and Bureaucratic Reform

As in other revolutions, after the Islamic revolution in Iran, ideological commitment rather than academic and technical expertise became the primary criterion for admittance into the bureaucratic and professional ranks. In addition, the revolution led to a massive exodus of professionals from government and other institutions. They were either expelled as part of a purification campaign or left because they found life under Islamic rule too rigorous. The resulting depletion of managerial, medical, and technical talent exacerbated Iran's perennial shortage of trained manpower. As with many other developing countries, and indeed, as was the case before the revolution, the problem is not so much the lack of top-level bureaucrats and managers as a shortage of mid-level experts. This situation is a major barrier to the success of the government's policy of reform and economic reconstruction.

To remedy this situation, the government needs to weed out untrained revolutionary zealots and to lure back Iranian professionals from inside the country and abroad. President Rafsanjani realizes this necessity, and in his speech to the parliament when introducing his cabinet, he emphasized the importance of professionalism and cultural and scientific regeneration for Iran's future. He called on Iranian professionals living abroad who were not, to use his word, traitors to return to Iran under his personal protection. Thus far, however, the government has had limited success. Why have only a few thousand Iranians so far returned?[25]

One answer is that the radicals oppose such a movement for ideological and material reasons. Knowing that a large-scale return of professionals is inconceivable without some easing of social and political restrictions, they have tried to discourage such a process. In the past, also, the radicals have successfully blocked government efforts to lure the exiles back. With President Rafsanjani's systematic efforts to reform the bureaucracy and encourage the return of the exiled experts, the complaints of the radicals have increased.

Another answer is that many exiles strongly feel they should not bail out a regime that they believe has grossly mistreated even those Iranians not politically identified with the Pahlavis. Even stronger, however, is their lack of confidence in the moderates' ability to ensure their safety.

Similar feelings exist among those Iranian professionals who could be characterized as "internal exiles." These people still live in Iran but refuse to cooperate with the regime. This attitude was described to me by an Iranian university professor living and working in Iran: "You created the mess; you deal with it." This point of view, however, is both shortsighted and destructive. The best hope for the peaceful evolution of Iran lies in the success of the moderates' policies, but success is not likely in the face of the radicals' sabotage and the professionals' lack of cooperation. This situation, however, could change quickly. If the moderates revitalize the economy and stabilize the political situation, a considerable number of exiles may return. As 1990 came to a close, in fact, when the first signs of Iran's economic revival became apparent and the moderate trend—especially President Rafsanjani's policy of national reconciliation—seemed to be on track, the outlook for the return of exiled professionals and entrepreneurs seemed more promising. By the end of 1991, however, obstruction had prevented a significant influx of Iranian exiles.

Reestablishment of Law and Order:
Reform of Internal Security Instruments

Iran's revolutionary decade has been characterized by considerable internal instability, the breakdown of law and order, and a widespread feeling of insecurity among the population. This situation has eroded business confidence. It has been responsible for the unwillingness of the business community to invest, the flight of capital, a brain drain, and the overall deterioration of the Iranian economy.

To restore the business and professional confidence essential for Iran's economic recovery, the problem of insecurity must be resolved. Postrevolutionary Iran has had two sources of insecurity. Its problems with insurgencies (ethnic, tribal, and other) have been one source. These problems are now almost resolved or at least are manageable. The other source has been the breakup of internal security forces and the proliferation of committees and other self-styled revolutionary organizations engaged in wide-ranging activities, from tracking the regime's political opponents to enforcing the Islamic dress code and other rules of conduct. Although it is difficult to judge the extent to which these committees have abused their authority, there is no doubt that they have done so extensively. Tales abound of their mistreatment of the population, including monetary extortions. But their more serious impact, as far as public confidence is concerned, has been a breakdown of the internal security apparatus, the multiplication of law enforcement agencies, and an overall confusion as to the real center of authority.

The Rafsanjani administration has been aware that as long as this situation is not remedied, the public's confidence could not be restored. Thus, the government has made efforts to coordinate the activities of various law enforcement agencies and bring them under the control and supervision of the Ministry of the Interior.

The most important measure in this regard was the creation of the Organization of Security Guards of the Islamic Republic of Iran by merging the gendarmerie, Islamic committees, and the police. This organization is to act as the executive arm of the judiciary. Its members are identified as the Security Guard Corps. Clause 8 of Article 4 of the bill establishing the organization lists the duties of the security force personnel as follows: fighting narcotics, contraband, forbidden deeds, corruption; preventing and detecting crime; inspecting and investigating; preserving evidence of crimes; arresting the accused and criminals and preventing their escape or their going into hiding; and enforcing judicial verdicts.[26]

Implementing this bill initially seemed a lengthy and difficult process. In particular, disciplining the most unruly members of the Islamic committees posed serious dilemmas. The government's strategy of incorporating the committees in a larger security body, thus preserving some of their material privileges rather than disbanding them altogether—helped in efforts to streamline law enforcement. The new unified force became operational in April 1991.

If successful, these reforms will help restore the people's sense of security and improve their willingness to heed the government's call to take a more active part in the country's economic and social reconstruction and revitalization. Although it will take some time for the rule of law to be established fully in Iran and for the people to feel secure, some progress has been made as the Rafsanjani administration has consolidated its position. Another encouraging development that could improve the human rights picture in Iran was the passage of a bill by the parliament in December 1990 that guarantees the right of all defendants to lawyers. If ratified by the 12-member Council of Guardians, the bill will force all civil, penal, military, and religious courts to accept the presence of lawyers chosen by the defendant in all stages of a case. Like all other positive developments in this regard, however, the test would come in fully implementing recent legislation in letter and in spirit.

2

The Military Establishment: Adapting to Peacetime

Background and Developments since the Revolution

By the time of the revolution, Iran's military strength was at its height, and its armed forces were among the best in the Third World. The military was also considered to be solidly behind the regime.[27] The latter, however, was proved only partially true when significant numbers of the military switched their loyalty from the king to the faqih. Despite this development, and the Ayatollah Khomeini's invitation to the military to join the revolution and the nation, however, the new regime remained suspicious of the armed forces as a hotbed of monarchist, nationalist, and pro-West tendencies. These suspicions were not totally unfounded because over the years several coup attempts involving segments of the military were carried out.

The antimilitary crusade of the new regime in the early days of the revolution was also encouraged by a variety of leftist forces, such as the Marxist Fedayan-e-Khalq and the Islamo-Marxist Mujaheddin-e-Khalq, that demanded complete dismantling of the armed forces and the creation of a people's army.[28] Although the Islamic regime did not completely dismantle the military, it embarked on a systematic

46

purge of the armed forces and the reeducation and Islamization of the military. It also created a parallel military
force in the form of the Islamic Revolutionary Guards
Corps (IRGC).[29]

Several factors saved the armed forces from complete
disintegration at the hands of the new regime. The most
important consideration was the security of the country,
which was threatened by both external and internal elements. Externally, the Soviet invasion of Afghanistan and
Iraqi subversion in Khusistan had created a sensitive situation. Internally, ethnic and tribal unrest made some level of
military preparedness essential. Another factor was disagreement within the Islamic leadership on how best to
handle the military. Some elements favored co-optation,
and others favored total purge. Despite these necessities
and reservations, one year after the revolution, Iran's armed
forces – with the possible exception of the navy – were muti-
lated and its command structure seriously undermined by
systematic purges and widespread desertions.

What rescued the regular armed forces from complete
demise was the Iran-Iraq War. Faced with the Iraqi invasion, the government of President Abol-Hassan Bani-Sadr
not only stopped the execution of top- and middle-level officers, but also called some of the air force officers out of
retirement.[30]

Forced to maintain some of the military, the government embarked on a large-scale Islamic indoctrination program for existing members of the military, new recruits,
and students in the military academies. It also drastically
expanded the IRGC into a parallel military force structured
like the regular armed forces with its own army, air force,
and naval units.

This fracturing of Iran's military establishment and
continued mistrust between the regular armed forces and
the Islamic leadership had extremely negative consequences for Iran, particularly during the crucial years of
war with Iraq. Article 110 of the 1979 constitution provided
for a Supreme Defense Council with both president and

prime minister, as well as the military commander from the regular forces and the IRGC, as members. These provisions proved inadequate, however, for proper command and control of the various military forces. Despite efforts to improve communications between the regular armed forces and the Revolutionary Guards and to develop a clear decision-making center on defense matters, the Iranian military's command and control problems continued for most of the 1980s. In 1987, with the war turning against Iran, a new body known as the Supreme Council for Support of the War Effort was created. In 1988, with further military setbacks, the Ayatollah Khomeini appointed the then-speaker of parliament, Hodjat-al-Islam Rafsanjani, as acting commander in chief and ordered the formation of a General Command of the Armed Forces, which was to coordinate actions of the army and the IRGC, merge parallel organizations, combine the resources of defense industries, enforce military laws, and punish offenders.

After hostilities ended between Iran and Iraq, the military's future, particularly the relationship between the regular armed forces and the IRGC, became an important concern. The role of the military in the country's political developments after the Ayatollah Khomeini's death was also in the minds of the Iranian leaders.

Regarding the relationship between the forces, the most important issue was whether the regular armed forces and the IRGC should be merged. A merger would consolidate their joint resources and centralize command and control. The IRGC, however, strongly resisted the idea of a merger. Its members were concerned that they would lose their identity — and privileges — in such a merger, and they feared, especially the high command, that they would become subordinate to the regular armed forces commanders.

Different factions also opposed a merger. They each had different links to the military that they had often used as leverage against one another in the intraregime rivalry for power. With uncertainties clouding the political future, none of them were willing to give up this leverage. With the smooth transition of power after the Ayatollah Khomeini's death, however, this factor has become less important, although it remains significant.

Suspicions regarding the depth of the regular armed forces' loyalty to the regime and their future political role, although much diminished, persist. Despite Islamization and co-optation of large segments of the regular forces, leftist or nationalist antiregime sentiments remain among the regular forces, especially the officer corps, but their strength is not easy to ascertain. Nevertheless, incidents such as the discovery of elements that allegedly had been passing vital military information to the United States during the Iran-Iraq War illustrate that the regime's suspicions are not unwarranted.[31]

As a result, the Rafsanjani administration did not initially push for the merger of military forces. It opted for a more gradual move in that direction by increasing cooperation between the IRGC and the regular forces. Two specific measures were intended to help this process. First, some of the top leadership of the IRGC and the regular forces are to be chosen from the other force. Second, more joint maneuvers and operations will take place between the IRGC forces and the regular armed forces. But as the moderates consolidated their position, they moved to merge the two forces. This was decided in the spring of 1991.

Implementing the decision proved difficult, however. The resistance of IRGC members succeeded in reversing the trend toward merging and integrating all military forces. By the end of 1991, the IRGC seemed to be consolidating itself into an elite military unit dedicated to defending the revolution. In this goal, the IRGC seemed to enjoy the support of the supreme leader. The IRGC's future is not necessarily settled, however. As previous trends toward merger were halted, the current trend could also be reversed. What is clear is that this issue will not be resolved before the tug of war between the moderates and the hardliners is settled.

The Role of the Military in Iranian
Society and Politics

Iran is different from most Middle Eastern countries in that its military has never played a significant political role in the country, despite the coup d'état of Reza Khan in 1921. This phenomenon is partly explained by Iran's history. Since the fall of the Sassanid empire in the seventh century A.D., standing military forces were never important; military forces were instead raised as the occasion required.

In the nineteenth century, when the foundations of the military establishments of other Middle Eastern countries were laid, two factors prevented the establishment of a viable military force in Iran: Iran's economic difficulties allied to the degenerate nature of its political leadership and the active discouragement of Britain and Russia.

The first and last effort at military modernization before the Pahlavis came to power was made by the Crown Prince Abbas Mirza Qajar during the first round of Russo-Iranian wars (1804–1813) with French help. France sent the first military advisers to Iran under the command of General Guardan.

Iran never had a military establishment with the strong esprit de corps that existed, for instance, in the Ottoman Empire and left a legacy throughout the Arab Middle East. Moreover, even after the military was set up in Iran on the model of modern military forces under the first Pahlavi king, the armed forces focused their loyalty on the monarch rather than on their own establishment.

Additionally, both Pahlavi kings, fearful of the challenge to their own power, systematically prevented strong-minded and popular military leaders from emerging. They also kept the military out of politics. The last shah, in particular, perfected this technique. This situation partly accounts for the military's paralysis during the 1978 crisis. Without the leadership of the king, the military was incapable of effective political action. Another consequence of the Pahlavis' attitude toward the military was that in the eyes of many Iranians, the military came to be seen not as a national institution that defended the nation's interests, but rather as the shah's private army and an instrument of popular repression.

Since the revolution, the Iranian military has changed considerably. First, it has become much more politicized, although it still is not a coherent political force that can act independently and decisively as can, for example, the Turkish, Pakistani, or Egyptian military establishments. Although politically more aware, Iran's military establishment is divided ideologically. For example, nationalist tendencies are still strongest among the regular armed forces.

The Revolutionary Guards, while committed to the regime, reflect intraregime philosophical and other differences. The failure of efforts to merge the two forces indicates that political differences within the military cannot be easily eliminated, and thus Iran's military forces will remain politically divided. The fragmentation of the Iranian military establishment reduces its ability to act decisively in the political arena. It also makes it easier for the civilian-religious leadership to control the military. In fact, under the Islamic leadership, civilian control of the military has been enhanced. This control is exercised through the spiritual leader (faqih), who is also the commander in chief, and the Supreme Defense Council. Nevertheless, in the political balancing act that has been going on in Iran in the last several years, the military and its various political proclivities have been important, albeit background, elements.

The popular image of the military has also undergone considerable changes. As a general rule, both the regular armed forces and the Revolutionary Guards have gained legitimacy in the public view because of their role in the Iran-Iraq War and their success in defending the country's territorial integrity, if not in winning a victory.

The popular view as to which of these forces contributed more to the nation's defense is divided. Judgment is influenced by political preferences. Thus, the more nationalistically inclined Iranians give most of the credit to the regular armed forces. In fact, they blame the government for having weakened the armed forces with purges and other restrictions, which encouraged Iraqi aggression and undermined Iran's performance in the war.

The regime itself and its supporters give most of the credit for resisting the Iraqis and maintaining the country's territorial integrity to the Revolutionary Guards. Overall, however, the military establishment is now more of a national institution and has a more positive image, despite a good deal of resentment among some of the population caused by the excesses of segments of the Revolutionary Guards during the early days of the revolution.

The role of the military in Iran will, to a great extent, be determined by the country's overall political development. If the Islamic regime continues to evolve in a moderate direction, broadening its popular support, developing a more balanced synthesis of the various aspects of Iran's cultural identity, and in general working toward a more broad-based national consensus, the Iranian military establishment will also become more integrated, cohesive, and representative.

Because such a process would strengthen Iran's political institutions, the military's role in Iran would come to resemble more that of the military in a democratic system, where the military is subject to civilian control and is not directly involved in politics. If the regime cannot reform itself and adapt to the requirements of an increasingly interdependent and complex world, Iran's internal divisions will deepen and the political postures of various groups will harden. In that scenario, the military establishment would certainly be drawn into the political dispute to determine the country's future.

The military's involvement in politics, however, is likely to bode ill for Iran, raising the specter of civil war, because the military is not a cohesive force. What is less and less likely, nevertheless, is a military coup d'état, be it of a nationalist or a radical variety, on the part of various elements of the armed forces. Some elements of the military, especially the Revolutionary Guards, may still become involved in an intraregime power struggle, especially in a plot against the moderates should they be perceived as going too far.

The Size of the Military Establishment

One of the most widely heard criticisms of the shah, both inside Iran and abroad, concerned his so-called obsessions with military strength and the disproportionate share of the national income spent on the military.

Domestically, criticism centered on the following two points: first, military expenditures took away funds from much-needed economic and social programs to improve the living conditions of the underprivileged segments of the society; and second, Iran did not face any security threat against which its military forces could be a credible deterrent or defense.

The critics of the shah's policy of military buildup dismissed regional threats to Iran's security. Regarding the Soviet threat, they argued that if the Soviet Union decided to invade Iran, Iran could not put up a credible defense anyway. They said the only protection against the Soviet threat was the global balance of power in the context of the East-West conflict and proper diplomacy. Thus, they argued that the military expenditures pampered the military, protected the Pahlavi regime, and acted as an instrument of domestic repression and a Western surrogate in the Persian Gulf against the vital interests of Iran and the majority of its people. Those elements – including the religious factions that brought down the shah – by and large shared in these views.

During the 1980s, however, a number of internal and regional events demonstrated to the Islamic leaders Iran's inherently unstable security environment and, hence, the necessity for a reasonable defense force. The most significant of these events was the Soviet invasion of Afghanistan in December 1979 and Iraq's aggression against Iran in September 1980. Since that time, Iran's Islamic leaders—as well as the majority of the people—have become convinced that Iran needs a strong defense force.

Immediately after the end of the war, there was some talk of reducing military expenditures and the number of men in arms. For several reasons, this kind of talk did not last long. First, the state of "no war, no peace" between Iran and Iraq and Iraq's vastly superior military power made such a course highly imprudent. Second, the regime soon became acutely aware of the potentially disastrous political consequences of antagonizing the military—especially the Revolutionary Guards—by cuts in its budget and personnel. Third, regional developments, especially those related to the Soviet Union's Asian empire and the Persian Gulf crisis, leading to the introduction of foreign forces to the region, created new threats.

Moreover, Iran's military, especially in equipment and training, is behind those of its immediate neighbors, such as Pakistan, Turkey, and, in some regards, even Saudi Arabia.[32] Iran needs to upgrade its military to restore a balance. Such an effort, however, faces two major constraints—financial and political. Defense would have to compete with other, more pressing economic needs. Politically, Iran is unlikely to obtain the equipment it needs to modernize its military forces without dramatically improving its relations with the West.

The Soviet Union, however, could be a source, as illustrated by the delivery of a squadron of MiG-29s in 1990.[33] The Soviet Union's rapid disintegration in 1991 following the failed hard-line coup attempt clouds the future of military relations between Iran and whatever ultimately replaces the Soviet Union. Given Russia's enormous needs for foreign exchange, however, the Russian Federation may continue to sell arms to Iran. Other potential sources of military equipment are China, North Korea, and Brazil, although the quality of their equipment is vastly inferior to that of the West, especially that of the United States.

The Persian Gulf crisis and talk of the permanent stationing of U.S. forces within the Gulf states have intensified Iran's security concerns and put more focus on rebuilding the country's defenses. This trend will be intensified if Iran is not included in regional arrangements and if outside forces such as Egypt and Turkey are brought into the region with U.S. encouragement and under the overall U.S. military umbrella.

Iran has also been trying to develop a domestic defense industrial base. It has made some progress, but again, even compared with a number of Third World countries including such Middle Eastern countries as Egypt, Turkey, Pakistan, and Iraq (before the war with the United States), Iran's defense industry is in its infancy. Given Iran's technological, financial, and managerial deficiencies, the near-term prospect for Iran's defense industry is not very bright. Indeed, faced with popular complaints about shortages of industrial and other goods, the Iranian government has recently decided to switch part of its heavy industrial production from defense to civilian needs.[34] In the future, if able, Iran will try to expand its indigenous defense-industrial base.

3

The Economy: From Boom to Bust to What?

Weaknesses of the Shah's Economic Policy

By the 1979 revolution, Iran had made considerable economic progress while committing a number of serious mistakes. In general, however, Iran's economy at the time of the revolution was far from balanced and self-sufficient. In fact, in 1978, Iran's economy was typical of many other Third World countries in that it was utterly dependent on the oil sector. Iran had a characteristically Third World single-commodity export economy, in which oil accounted for more than 90 percent of its foreign exchange receipts and the oil sector accounted for nearly 50 percent of its gross national product (GNP).

The drive toward industrialization, which led to greater urbanization, left the agricultural sector neglected. Given such added factors as increased population growth and consumption, Iran had become a major food importer by the time of the revolution. In 1978, for example, Iran imported more than $2 billion worth of foodstuffs, meat, and dairy products.

Although the living standards of almost all segments of Iranian society had improved, the income distribution gap remained alarmingly large. This situation, together with the rise in social and political consciousness, had led to rising expectations that fueled popular dissatisfaction despite significant economic gains. Popular criticism of the shah's economic policy focused on the following points, discussed here because they indicate trends the Islamic regime would later try to reverse.

Waste of Oil Wealth

A cornerstone of the shah's economic policy was that Iran should transform its oil wealth into viable economic, especially industrial, power as quickly as possible. Thus, Iran should produce and export as much oil as it could as fast as it could, investing the earnings in industrial development. Under this policy, Iran's oil production capacity stood at 6 million barrels a day by 1979. The opposition's view, by contrast, was that Iran should preserve and extend the life of its oil reserves. Oil production should not exceed 3 million barrels a day.

Sham Industrialization

The shah's opponents believed that his industrialization policy was a sham because it did not create the sort of industries—notably heavy industries—that would make Iran truly independent and self-sufficient. The assembling of cars and other such items, they argued, could not be considered industrialization.

Opponents thus favored the building up of the heavy industrial sector. The leftist opposition, influenced by the socialist countries' experience, was especially enthusiastic in this regard. Indeed, it is interesting to note that for a long time the revolutionary regime's minister of heavy industries would be an ex-Tudeh member, Behzad Nabavi.

Neglect of Agricultural and Rural Areas and Regional Disparities

A significant complaint of the shah's opponents was that his policies had led to degradation of the agricultural sector and the neglect of rural areas. The revitalization of agriculture and the achievement of food self-sufficiency by 1991 would become the primary objective of the new regime.

The regime's opponents also rightly criticized the imbalance in the economic development of various provinces, leaving some of them far behind the rest of the country. Thus, another declared priority of the new regime was to remedy this imbalance and improve the condition of the so-called deprived areas.

Income Gap and Social Inequalities

Although the living standards of nearly all sectors of the Iranian population had vastly improved by 1978, the economic and social gap had widened. According to some estimates, by 1978, 30 percent of the income-receiving households received almost 90 percent of the total household income.[35]

There were also significant disparities between urban and rural areas and among different provinces. These relative disparities, rather than improvement in overall living conditions, became the focus of popular attention and complaint. All opposition groups called for an end to these economic and social disparities and the creation of a classless society, whether secular or Islamic.

Ideological Confusion: Impediment to Economic Planning and Development

Philosophical differences and ideological confusion among opposition groups and within the Islamic forces concerning the nature of Iran's economic system have been a primary reason why the revolutionary regime has failed in the economic sphere.

First, none of the opposition forces, with the possible exception of the secular left, concentrated on developing a coherent conceptual and operational framework for Iran's

economic development. All were quick to criticize the existing policies, with some justification, but none offered realistic alternatives.

A thorough technical knowledge of economics, as it related to Iran's own conditions and to the international environment, was not a strong point of opposition leaders either. Even the thinking of such figures as Abol-Hassan
Bani-Sadr, who had pretensions in this regard and wrote
about their vision of an Islamic economic system or Eghte-
sad-e-Towhidi (monotheistic economics), was confused and
unfocused.

The Ayatollah Khomeini viewed economics as unim-
portant. In general, the opposition's thinking on economics
was simplistic and dominated by a few fundamental concepts and premises reflecting the influence of three strands
of thought.

Egalitarianism, Populism

In egalitarian or populist thought, an economic system
must create a classless and egalitarian society. The system
must be run through the active participation of people at all
levels of decision making and implementation.

Although often justified on the basis of Islamic principles, as in Abol-Hassan Bani-Sadr's concept of monotheistic economics, for example, or the Ayatollah Khomeini's
own vision of protecting the rights of the "Mustazefin" (the
deprived), this strand reflects the impact of leftist ideas and
the utopian vision of a classless society.

Self-Reliant Development

In one form or another, all opposition thinkers bemoaned
Iran's economic dependence on what they considered to be
the imperialist Western industrial nations. They called for
an economic development strategy to end this state of
dependency.

In the context of this theory, the multinational corporations were considered particular villains. Extending this thinking to the domain of Iran's international economic ties led most opposition figures to call for Iran to downgrade its ties with the West and expand its relations with Third World countries. These ideas, however, are not novel; they represent the thinking of most Third World intellectuals and some European leftists in the 1960s and the 1970s. They are derivatives of the dependency theory of international economics popular in the Third World and at the root of such terms as "collective self-reliance" and "South-South cooperation" that were current in Third World and UN parlance long before the Iranian revolution.

The interesting point is that by the time of the revolution, these ideas had lost much of their validity and credibility even among Third World intellectuals and governments.

Satisfying Social Needs versus Economic Growth

The thinking of Iranian revolutionaries reflects the impact of another Third World intellectual trend of the 1970s—namely, the view that satisfying basic social needs (health, education, housing, and so on), rather than achieving high growth rates, should be the object of economic development. It is generally agreed that growth without attention to social needs is not desirable. It is difficult, however, to envisage how these needs can be satisfied without adequate and balanced economic growth.

The State as a Principal Economic Actor

Even before the revolution, the state had played an important, if not central, role in Iran's economic planning and development.[36] Most Iranians did not have any difficulty in accepting a central role for the state in the country's economic life. Within both secular and Islamic opposition, many believed in increasing the state's role in Iran's economy and extending state control to areas—foreign trade, for example — that had been mostly in private hands. Those in the opposition differed, however, on the extent of state control and the role of the private sector. The left — both Islamic and secular — favored total state control, while the non-left opposition favored a mixed economy. Within Islamic opposition groups, confusion was more extensive and differences were deeper.

Islamic Economics: Is It Possible?

Logically, an Islamic government must also have an Islamic economic system. The thinking of Iran's Islamic leaders on this subject, however, was even less advanced than on the political aspects of an Islamic government. Islamic injunctions on the economic life of Muslim societies are ambiguous and thus subject to various interpretations.

First, there is the tension between, on the one hand, Islam's sanctioning of the individual's right to property and to the fruits of his labor and, on the other hand, the notion that everything in this world belongs to God and that man can have it only as a trustee.

As one author has put it, the latter notion implies that a state representing the will of God can limit the individual's property rights for the protection of the highest good.[37] Applied to modern economic conditions, such interpretations could provide an Islamic justification for extensive state interference in the economy. There is, furthermore, a dimension to Islam's approach to issues of economic activity and social justice that, if not totally egalitarian, is very similar to principles underpinning the modern welfare state.

The Islamic system of taxation, for example, is designed to prevent vast social gaps. Moreover, Islam, through the institution of "Beit-al-Mal" (public treasury), assigns specific duties to the government to provide for the widows and orphans, and, in general, the needy.

In essence, therefore, Islam prescribes an economic system that could be described as "capitalism with a social conscience," a system where individual initiative is balanced by limited state intervention to protect the greatest good and the rights of society's more vulnerable sectors.

Thus, the interpretation of Islamic injunctions on economics has been disputed in Iran and other Muslim countries for reasons other than inherent contradictions in the Islamic theory of economics. The most important reason is that historically in the Muslim world, those aspects of Islamic principles dealing with social justice have been largely ignored. Indeed, in many Muslim countries, and certainly in Iran, many of the highest-ranking clerics have belonged to, or have been affiliated with, rich landowning and merchant families.

Moreover, the fortunes of many other clerics have traditionally depended on the same sources, and they behave accordingly. For example, the violent opposition of Iran's clerical establishment to land reform in 1963 was partly determined by these factors. Indeed, because of this situation, there has long been a widespread anticlerical feeling among segments of Iran's lower classes and intelligentsia, including those otherwise committed to Islam, as the views of the modern Iranian political theoretician Ali Shariati illustrate.

The second reason relates to the interaction between Islam and leftist ideologies in the last four decades. Leftist ideologies influenced the thinking of Muslim intellectuals and clerics, which led some of them to adopt a very liberal interpretation of the Islamic notions discussed above and to give their particular vision of Islamic society and economy a decidedly socialist character. In addition, Muslim clerics feared that socialism could threaten Islam as a focus of popular allegiance. Believing that socialism's appeal to the masses derived from its egalitarian dimensions, many 'Ulama' began to emphasize those same dimensions in Islam. The Ayatollah Muhammad Baqir As-Sadr, leader of the Iraqi Shi'as, penned his treatise on Islamic economics largely because of his concern about the growing influence

of the Communists over Iraq's impoverished and underprivileged Shi'as. Reportedly, even Iran's clerical leaders warned
the Ayatollah Khomeini while he was in exile in Najaf of the
spread of leftist ideas among Muslim youths.[38] In a parallel
phenomenon, certain leftists, recognizing Islam's hold on
the impoverished, uneducated classes incapable of understanding Marxist theories, cloaked their ideas in Islamic
terms and symbols. The result was growing confusion
about the interpretation of Islamic injunctions on economic
matters and greater polarization between socialistic and
capitalist interpretations of Islamic notions.

The Islamic regime has since been bedeviled by this
legacy of so-called Islamic economics. As the foregoing has
illustrated, however, the dichotomy between these two dimensions of Islamic thinking on economics has had less to
do with Islam than with the clash of class interests and the
influence of non-Islamic ideological thinking.

In practice, the Islamic regime's survival has thus far
depended on maintaining the support of its two constituencies—the merchant class and the traditional clergy, and the
lower classes—with vastly different aspirations and interests. This necessity has led to a policy of maintaining a
balance of power between their representatives within the
leadership. On the economic front, this policy has proven
disastrous, as the following examples illustrate.

Confusing Signals

The practice of maintaining a rough balance of power between the two principal factions within the Iranian leadership, together with periodic shifts in their relative influence, caused the government to send conflicting signals
regarding the respective roles of government and the private sector in the running of the country's economy. Generally, however, occasional encouragement to the private sector would be accompanied by stern warnings against
profiteering and admonishments to protect the interests of
the deprived.

This inconsistency stemmed from the Ayatollah Khomeini's attitude. His own inclination on economic matters was more in line with the more revolutionary and unorthodox interpretation of Islam. He was unwilling, however, to antagonize the powerful merchant community and the more traditionally oriented clerical figures. To keep both happy, the Ayatollah Khomeini filled the Council of Guardians, the body that determines the compatibility of legislation with Islamic law, with traditionalist clerics. Doing so balanced the radicals, who had a majority in the parliament and were widely represented within the executive branch. This situation led to a virtual legislative impasse; the Council of Guardians kept overturning parliamentary legislation on such key issues as land reform.[39] Meanwhile, amid this legislative deadlock and ideological confusion, the radical trend exerted the greatest influence on the country's overall economic environment and the government's economic policies through the following processes.

Revolutionary Institutions and Popular Committees

While the debate on the ideological foundations of the country's economic system and the legislative deadlock continued, Iran's economic structure acquired a de facto populist-radical bent. At one level, immediately after the revolution, there were large-scale nationalizations of industries and takeovers of plants and other property left vacant because their owners fled. In a parallel development, a variety of workers' councils and committees mushroomed throughout the country, making the management of remaining private enterprises nearly impossible. This further accelerated the flight of capital and entrepreneurial and managerial talent that would prove very costly for the country's economic future. Simultaneously, a number of Islamic and populist-oriented organizations such as the Reconstruction Crusade (Jehad-e-Sazandeghi) and the Foundation for the Deprived (Bonyad-e-Mustazefin) were created to fill the vacuum. Under the right circumstances, these new organizations could have done considerable good. But the lack of technical and managerial experience, institutional rivalry, and corruption seriously undermined their effectiveness.

War and Growing Government Control

In addition, the Iran-Iraq War and its consequences (such as rationing food and putting the economy on a war footing) led to increased governmental control of the economy. The combination of these factors gravely undermined business confidence; thus, very few people were willing to invest in productive activities. Consequently, the available capital was used in currency and real estate speculation that created their own problems.

The First Economic Development Plan

The first postrevolution development plan, presented in 1983, resembles a political manifesto more than an economic plan. Nevertheless, it is the only document that states the new regime's principal economic objectives and, hence, is the only benchmark against which to measure the government's performance. The plan states its principal objectives as the following:

1. Expand education and culture, ultimately leading to free primary and secondary education.
2. Secure economic independence, defined as the ability to provide locally the "capital goods, technology, and expertise" and on trading, manufacturing, and other locally produced goods rather than exporting mineral wealth such as oil.
3. Provide social security, health care, medical care, food, clothing, and housing.
4. Eliminate unemployment and secure the interests of the deprived.

How does the government expect to achieve these objectives? Again the plan's prescriptions sound more like ideological slogans than concrete and realistic steps:

- Prevent consumerism and emphasize investment
- Make agriculture the vanguard of the country's economic growth
- Expand research, which is considered essential for acquiring the scientific and technological base necessary for economic independence
- Train skilled personnel
- Expand secondary activities (that is, establish small industries) to raise the villagers' and tribespeople's income
- Establish links between various economic sectors
- Emphasize expansion of intermediate and machine tool industries
- Expand non-oil exports
- Prevent the expansion of large cities
- Use and maintain machinery
- Protect the environment.

The plan envisaged an annual gross domestic product (GDP) growth rate of 8 percent over its lifetime. In addition, the plan intended to deal with inflation and restore budgetary and fiscal balance. Beyond the recitation of these general objectives, however, the plan did not indicate how the government intended to achieve these goals.[40]

A principal flaw of the plan is that it was based on the assumption of an ever-rising oil income. There does not seem to have been any accounting for the war burden or any assessment of how long the war would last. This oversight is an unpardonable lapse; by the time the plan was finished, Iran was already three years into the war.

What is clear is that none of the plan's objectives were achieved. Indeed, because of political chaos, the lack of expert planning and implementation, and the devastation caused by the war, Iran is in a worse position today than it was in 1978. With a rapidly growing population—partly a legacy of the Islamic regime's policies—the tasks of building a self-sustaining economy for Iran and meeting the basic economic and social needs of its people loom even more daunting today than they did a decade ago.

Current Characteristics of the Economy

Continued Dependence on Oil

Despite the regime's emphasis on self-sufficiency, Iran's economy is still highly dependent on oil, although the oil industry's share in the country's overall gross national product (GNP) has declined. This has not been because of increased production in other sectors, however; rather, there has been a dramatic reduction in oil production and oil-related industries largely as a result of the Iran-Iraq War and its devastation.

This dependency on oil is even more acute when measured in terms of the percentage of oil income that makes up Iran's overall foreign exchange earnings. Even today, earnings from oil sales account for 90 percent of its overall export earnings. The earnings from non-oil exports, despite the government's efforts, have not exceeded the annual $1 billion mark by much. In addition, the composition of Iran's non-oil exports has remained unchanged, consisting mainly of such traditional items as nuts, carpets, dried fruit, hides, caviar, textiles, and footwear.

In short, Iran has not been able to diversify its export base. Moreover, inadequate investment, political chaos, and war damage have prevented Iran from becoming an exporter of, or at least self-sufficient in, such items as petrochemicals, fertilizers, and other oil derivatives. The underdeveloped state of Iran's petrochemical industry has also dampened the expansion of other industries, such as textiles, particularly those using synthetic fabrics.

Agricultural Dependency

Despite the government's goal of agricultural sufficiency, Iran still depends on imported foodstuffs. Iran annually imports around $2 billion worth of wheat, rice, meat, and dairy products, roughly the same amount as in 1978 despite a population increase. This has been more the result of a fall in consumption than an increase in domestic production. Indeed, with the availability of more resources, Iran's agricultural imports could top the $4 billion mark.

Some of the reasons for the lack of growth in the agricultural sector existed before the revolution. Others have been the result of revolutionary confusion and financial difficulties created by the war.

Moreover, whatever growth has been achieved in the agricultural sector has been more than absorbed by rapid population growth. Lack of adequate water for irrigation and uncertain rainfall have been long-standing problems for the development of Iran's agriculture. With adequate investment in building dams and harnessing the water that is wasted or, even worse, that periodically destroys crops and entire villages with flooding, Iran could have coped with its water problem. Even now, Iran uses only 58 million cubic meters of the total 135 million cubic meters of water available.[41] Under the shah's regime, a number of dams were built, and others were planned.[42]

The Islamic regime also has had plans for dam building—especially small dams, which are as important, if not more so, than larger dams. Preoccupation with the Iran-Iraq War, financial constraints caused by the war, and falling oil prices have thwarted these goals.

The low technological base of Iran's agriculture has been another long-standing problem. Even today, most of Iran's agriculture is done with traditional methods, because mechanization and the introduction of high-yield seeds have not gone very far. Again, both before and after the revolution, not enough attention was paid to upgrading the technological basis of Iranian agriculture.

The landownership regime and the mishandling of this

issue, especially the inability to strike a proper balance between the need to give land to the peasants and economic
efficiency, have contributed to Iran's agricultural woes. After the revolution, ideological divisions within the regime
on land reform exacerbated this long-standing problem.

The high rate of illiteracy among the peasantry and the
lack of an adequate social infrastructure in the villages have
also hampered agricultural growth. It is much more difficult to introduce mechanization and high-tech agriculture
to illiterate peasants. Past efforts at educating the rural
population were never sufficient or very effective. Iran's
large size, the dispersion of villages, and the large distances
between them have made the task of building a rural social
infrastructure very daunting.

In addition to these fundamental problems, both before
and after the revolution, faulty planning contributed to
Iran's agricultural difficulties in the pre- and post-revolution period. Since the revolution, bureaucratic difficulties,
especially the multitude of ministries and agencies involved
in agricultural planning and implementation, have hampered agricultural development.

In short, despite the proclaimed intentions of the Islamic regime to make the agricultural sector the vanguard
of Iran's economic development, neither the state of Iran's
agriculture nor the living standards of its peasants have
improved much in the last 10 years, although some progress
has been made in rural electrification and road-building.
Indeed, because of the war, entire villages in some regions
have been erased.

Iran's agricultural potential, however, is significant.
Given adequate investment and proper utilization of resources, it can meet the bulk of its food needs and increase
its agricultural exports.

Reducing the Economic and Social Gap

The economic and social gap could be reduced in two ways:
by cutting the income of the privileged through expropriation and high taxation and distributing the balance among

the poor; or by increasing output and directing the new wealth generated to the less advantaged segments of society through higher wages or shares in the companies and the provision of adequate and affordable social services such as health, education, and recreation.

The Islamic regime thus far has chosen the first route. Through expropriation and nationalization, the regime has reduced the income of the upper echelon of Iranian society. Initially, there were wage increases for workers and some civil servants. The economic downturn caused by the war, falling oil income, and faulty policies, has, however, impoverished the entire population. Living standards have fallen across the board, with the very poor, the civil service, and other fixed-income categories suffering most.

Even though the economic gap leveled off somewhat during the first years of the new regime, a new rich class has emerged in Iran. The wealth of this new class is the result of manipulating the black market, hoarding, and speculating in land and currency. The emergence of this new rich class has accentuated the polarization of Iranian society between a small, very rich minority and the overwhelming majority of the poor. Moreover, the exploding population and widespread impoverishment have dramatically increased the percentage of those Iranians living at or below the poverty line.[43] At the root of the regime's inability to close the gap has been the inherent deficiency of a purely distributive strategy. Such a strategy cannot create a more balanced income distribution as can a method based on economic growth and an equitable tax system. The debate on the merits of a redistributive versus growth-based strategy for reducing income disparities is likely to continue in Iran. Without overall economic growth, however, the conditions of Iran's deprived people probably will not improve much. The Rafsanjani administration's awareness of the importance of economic growth to Iran's overall prosperity gives reason for optimism that Iran may finally be able to strike a balance between economic growth and economic and social equity.

The Iranian regime has failed to create an economically more prosperous and egalitarian society, but on the social level, its populist philosophy has led to a more representative and less elitist society, reflecting the mass rather than elite culture. For example, the Islamic dress code does more than protect Islamic morality. To some extent, it hides economic and social distinctions. Also, being modern and Westernized is no longer a sign of distinction and no excuse for a minority to slight the values and customs of the majority of the people.

This situation has had an important psychological impact. It has provided emotional, if not economic, satisfaction for the masses and initially eased their disappointment at the lack of material gains. But growing economic hardship has diluted this satisfaction.

Industrial Stagnation and Continued
Import Dependency

Another grievance of the opposition to the shah was that Iran, after several decades of experimenting with industrial development, still depended on imports of technology and industrial goods to a degree that was neither economically nor politically sound.

Consequently, achieving industrial and technological self-sufficiency was one of the principal goals of the revolutionary regime's economic policy. As in so many other areas, this goal, too, fell victim to the effects of war, political uncertainty, and economic mismanagement. Indeed, as a result of war damage, the lack of raw materials, and foreign currency shortages, not only were there no increases in Iran's industrial capacity, but by 1988 Iran's industries were operating at less than 40 percent of their capacity.

The Islamic government has tried to encourage indigenous research to improve the country's technological capabilities. And, in fact, in some areas (especially in the military field), the Iranians have demonstrated considerable ingenuity and adaptability. Advances in this regard, however, have been much less significant than can be concluded from the Iranian press reports of technological feats by Iranian scientists and engineers. One factor behind the disappointing results in the pursuit of technological self-sufficiency has been the migration of many technical experts and Iran's serious brain drain.

Regional Disparities

Despite certain administrative reforms aimed at encouraging economic development at the regional level with the specific goal of improving the lot of the least-developed regions, regional disparities have remained unchanged. Indeed, with the overall economic downturn, damage inflicted by the war, and natural disasters, many previously prosperous regions, such as Khusistan, have been reduced to the status of least-developed regions.[44]

War Damage

The eight-year war with Iraq has set back Iran's development for at least two decades. Moreover, the damage done to Iran's economic infrastructure and the psychological health of its people has exacerbated many of its traditional developmental problems.

The 1980s was a lost decade in terms of Iran's development. During this period, the money that should have been invested in developing Iran's human and material infrastructure financed the war instead. The cost of financing the war for Iran has been estimated at $5 billion annually. This amount is nearly half of Iran's oil income for the period of 1980–1988. In other words, Iran has lost $40 billion of its oil income on war. Even at the minimal return on investment of 5 percent annually, without compounding, Iran would have earned $2 billion annually, which puts the total lost income at $56 billion.

Damage to the oil fields has added to the loss of income. The lack of investment in maintaining the fields, the prolonging of their life through gas reinjection and other techniques, and the destruction of existing fields, offshore platforms, and export terminals have reduced the productive life of Iranian oil fields and have left a huge need for financial resources to revitalize the oil industry.

The damage to the oil fields is hard to quantify in dollars. But if it is assumed that Iran has lost five years of annual production of 3 million barrels a day at an average price of $15 per barrel, the total loss is approximately $75 billion. If one adds the conservative estimate of nearly $20 billion needed to revitalize Iran's oil industry, the total cost of misused and lost oil income to Iran as a result of the war amounts to $95 billion.

In addition, nearly all industrial plants, agricultural facilities, communication centers, and so forth were damaged during the war. The damage done to these sectors, according to a 1983 government report, is estimated at $199 billion. Given the fact that massive Iraqi air attacks worsened after 1983, this estimate should be increased. In fact, a 1985 government report increased this estimate to approximately $309 billion. What is important to note is that these estimates do not include damage done to military establishments. In short, by computing the lost income and various damages, a rough estimate of $500 billion in war damages is a reasonable figure. In a recent speech at a conference on Iran's reconstruction, President Rafsanjani put the direct war damage at $600 billion and the total cost at $1 trillion.[45]

In addition to material damages, the war has destroyed the social fabric of many communities, turning their inhabitants into refugees living in temporary housing with government assistance. The task of resettling these refugees in their ancestral dwellings and providing them with jobs and social services is daunting. The war has also left the country with 1.7 million handicapped people who must be cared for.

In assessing the social and psychological impact of the war, however, the following point needs to be made. The war has contributed to a sense of national wholeness in the country and has brought most Iranians closer together. Iranians from different regions, who under normal circumstances would have never come in contact with one another, fought in trenches together for the same homeland. Indeed, as one Iranian professor told me, there is hardly a village in Iran that does not have a war martyr's grave with an Iranian flag flying over it.

Economic Prospects: Challenges and Assets

The foregoing estimates about the damage done to Iran's economy by the war illustrate the magnitude of the task that faces the Iranian government of revitalizing and developing Iran's economy and of meeting the frustrated expectations of its long-suffering people. This already gigantic challenge was further aggravated by the devastating earthquake that hit parts of northern and northwestern Iran on June 21, 1990. The damage done by the earthquake is estimated to be $7 billion.[46] In tackling this task, Iran's leaders are faced with four especially thorny problems.

Demographic Explosion. One of Iran's principal short- and long-term developmental problems is the high rate of population growth. Since the revolution, the growth rate has measured somewhere between 3.5 percent to 3.9 percent annually. Indeed, it is estimated that Iran's population could surpass the 100 million mark by the end of the year 2006.

Moreover, like other Third World countries, Iran's population is very youthful. Nearly 50 percent of Iran's population is 15 or younger. Such a young and growing population tremendously strains the government's ability to provide housing, education, health services, and jobs. It is estimated that 600,000 people enter the job market annually, which makes reducing the rate of unemployment a gigantic task.[47]

Population control measures applied soon and effectively will be necessary to ease these pressures. But even the most effective population control measures will take a long time to stabilize the growth rate. A positive note in this regard, however, is that the Iranian authorities and religious leaders are aware of the necessity of population control. Indeed, the notion popular early in the revolution that a larger population would help Iran to propagate its ideology has lost its appeal.

On the contrary, the Iranian authorities have been promoting the theme that what is important is to have Islamic communities that are economically prosperous and socially just rather than to have sheer numbers. Indeed, one religious leader at one point expressed the view that large numbers of hungry Muslims with their hands outstretched to foreigners are not going to serve the interests of the Islamic world.[48]

Although government has begun an educational campaign on birth control and has been providing free contraceptive devices, its efforts have been hampered by the lack of adequate supplies of devices stemming from a shortage of foreign currency. Once Iran's foreign currency resources improve and the needed material is available, these policies will have a better chance of success.

Unemployment and Its Ills. Like most other Third World countries, Iran has had a perennial problem of unemployment and underemployment. This problem has acquired gigantic proportions since the revolution as a result of economic stagnation and demographic pressures. The official rate of unemployment is 14 percent. The real figure for unemployment and underemployment is much higher, as indicated by the second five-year development plan, which states as one of its goals the reduction of unemployment to 14 percent by 1993.[49]

Thus, the provision of jobs for a growing population is a vitally important task of the government. Such a high level of unemployment, if not reduced, could mean social disaster for Iran and a political nightmare for the government. Moreover, the many unemployed youth could become a very serious liability for the regime because they could be manipulated by its internal and external opponents.

The scarcity of jobs, the lack of adequate sports and recreational facilities, and the hardships and anxieties of the war have led to a rise in drug addiction among Iranian youth. The problem of drug addiction is not a novel phenomenon in Iran. Nor is it the only Islamic country in this predicament. Pakistan and Egypt, for example, also have a severe drug addiction problem.[50] The large number of those using hard drugs such as heroin, however, even when adjusted for population increase, is very disturbing.

The government has been aware of this problem and has periodically launched antidrug campaigns. Because of the factors noted above and because of extensive cultivation and smuggling of drugs in Iran's neighboring areas, especially Afghanistan and Pakistan, these policies have not been very effective.

The Shortage of Capital. The devastation wrought on Iran by the war and the earthquake, the necessity of increasing output in every sector of the economy, and the large volume of imports needed for economic reconstruction mean that Iran's capital and foreign exchange needs are staggering. It is estimated, for example, that Iran will need $27 billion in foreign exchange beyond its export earnings to implement its new five-year development plan.

In theory, Iran should not have much trouble gaining access to capital. Iran is one of the very few Third World countries with a high rate of creditworthiness; it has little long-term foreign debt. With its oil and gas reserves and other resources, Iran's ability to service a reasonable amount of foreign debt is quite good. Thus, under the right circumstances, Iran should be able to borrow from both international development and lending institutions and from private international banks. There is also a considerable pool of Iranian capital abroad that under the right cir-

cumstances, could be attracted to Iran. Moreover, businessmen residing in Iran have foreign currency holdings that
could be siphoned into the economy.

Attracting the needed capital is a political problem for
the Iranian regime. First, there is the disagreement within
the Iranian leadership on the issue of foreign borrowing.
This disagreement is compounded by manipulation of this
issue in intraregime infighting. Iranian radicals particularly
fear that external borrowing would again lead to Iran's political domination by foreigners because the West controls
the capital resources. This would mean Western dominance,
which strikes a sensitive chord in the Iranians' psyche.
Iran's recent history has been replete with instances when
foreign borrowing has led to foreigners' receiving undue
concessions and privileges.[51] Those who argue against excessive borrowing are not totally wrong, as the case of the
Third World's big debtors illustrates.

The issue of foreign borrowing, however, has become
one of the principal weapons with which the radicals have
tried to sabotage President Rafsanjani's economic recovery
strategy.

Yet, despite the traditional Iranian revulsion against
foreign borrowing and the radicals' opposition, the necessity of some borrowing has been recognized. Initially a compromise was reached limiting foreign borrowing to those
projects that, once completed, would be self-financing. Later, the government was forced to apply for emergency loans
for the reconstruction of areas damaged by the earthquake.
In fact, the World Bank granted a $250 million emergency
loan to Iran for this purpose. Moreover, Iran is interested in
getting World Bank loans for major infrastructural projects, including the building of a third dam on the Karun
River in Khusistan province.[52] But there seems to be greater reluctance to borrow from the IMF, even among the moderates; the IMF's rules of conditionality imply considerable
supervision of and interference in the country's economic
policies.

Psychological and political barriers are also still strong

in the case of private foreign investment. Economic necessities, however, are weakening these obstacles. Iranian capital may be more acceptable. Here, too, business confidence in the political stability of the country and predictability of the government's economic policies must first be restored. Some radicals also fear that the return of Iranian and Western capital implies the return of political and cultural influences prevalent before the revolution. There is strong evidence, however, that the government is plannig to restore the nationalized industries to those owners who were not too closely identified with the shah's regime.[53] Meanwhile, the government has set up a free trade zone in the Persian Gulf island of Qishm, where foreign investment would be encouraged. And, in general, both economic and social policies on the island would be much more liberal than those on the mainland.[54] Iran's success or failure in attracting expatriate and foreign capital will depend on whether President Rafsanjani and his moderate colleagues prevail and overcome the radicals' opposition and obstructions.

Inflation and Exchange Rate Chaos.   High rates of inflation have been a principal problem of the Iranian economy since the revolution, although inflationary pressures were strong and growing throughout the 1970s. The prerevolutionary inflation was the symptom of an overheated economy and the result of frenzied spending during the oil-boom days. Inflation after the revolution was accompanied by an economic slowdown. Indeed, Iran's economic situation has been one of stagflation, similar, albeit more severe, to that experienced by some European countries in the 1970s. Inflation has particularly hit such fixed-income categories as civil servants — who have not had any significant wage increases. Retirees have suffered most.

The principal causes of inflation in Iran have been low production levels, supply shortages, hoarding, black-marketeering, and governmental inability to control the black market. In the past, the government response has been to threaten the hoarders and black marketeers with punishment.

It is very difficult to determine Iran's real rate of inflation. Official figures have vacillated in the teens and the twenties during the last decade. According to the latest government statistics, for example, the inflation rate was 23.70 percent in 1986–1987, 27.70 percent in 1987–1988, and 28.98 percent in 1988–1989. There is reason to believe that the real rate of inflation has been higher than official figures. The accumulated rate of inflation since the revolution is at times estimated as high as 400 percent. The problem of inflation is unlikely to be resolved until the supply situation is rectified.

Housing prices, both for rent and purchase in particular, have skyrocketed. The government argues, however, that because 80 percent of the population own their houses, high housing prices are not a significant hardship.

Another of the government's significant problems is the need to rationalize the exchange rate and close the gap between the official and black-market rate of the rial to the dollar and other major currencies. Without rationalizing the exchange rate, Iran's ability to borrow from abroad, especially from such institutions as the IMF, is undermined.

Even before the revolution, the ratio of the rial to the dollar was unbalanced, with the rial being overvalued. This imbalance has become exceedingly serious. Part of this situation can be explained by the overall economic downturn. Part of the problem has been political, particularly fear over the war and a rush by many Iranians to buy dollars and other foreign currencies, either because they were leaving the country or as insurance against future problems. Speculators have also contributed to the rial's declining value. Overall, the shortage of foreign exchange and the government's inability to provide enough foreign exchange at the official rates have widened the gap between the official and black-market rates.

On the plus side, Iran has vast mineral resources, adequate water and agricultural land, and a reasonably literate labor force. With proper planning and harnessing of these resources, it should be able to experience satisfactory growth rates and improved living conditions. In fact, Iran's major economic problems also stem from political causes, most notably from obstruction by the radicals.

Rafsanjani's Economic Policies and Plans

The Rafsanjani administration's principal concerns immediately after being approved by the parliament in August 1989 were to ease some of the shortages of consumer goods and to increase domestic production. The government wanted to restore the industry's production to full capacity before increasing output or setting up new industries. The administration's efforts, however, were marred by the lack of foreign exchange, the difficulty of finding advantageous financing, the fall in oil prices, and the squabble within the leadership over foreign borrowing.

As a result of these constraints, the government's efforts during its first year did not dramatically improve either the average Iranian's living conditions or industrial production. Nevertheless, some improvements were achieved in both areas because government spending on the import of food, medicine, and other consumer products increased. Spending on industrial reconstruction also increased and resulted in higher output. The repair of the oil industry, including petrochemical plants, was one of the government's priorities. This rehabilitation started even before the Rafsanjani government was installed. The success rate of this work has been quite encouraging. For example, the first phase of the reconstruction of the Abadan refinery – the largest in the country before the Iraqis destroyed it – was completed in early 1989, and it began exporting petrochemical products in late 1989.[55] Other refineries in the rest of the country, such as those of Shiraz and Tabriz, were refurbished and by late 1990 were operating above their full capacity.[56]

The repair of power stations that had been very badly damaged, causing blackouts and brownouts, was also a priority, although progress in this arena has been slower. Even as of late 1990, the overall performance of the industrial sector was only 50 percent of full capacity. But by the fall of 1991, statements by Iranian officials put the industry's output at 85 percent of capacity.

As part of its policy of industrial reinvigoration, the Rafsanjani administration has tried to attract private investment; it decided that between 500 and 800 industrial concerns would be sold to the public. This policy, however, has not met with total success. Part of the problem has been the obstructions of the hard-liners who have suggested that the investors buying these industries should allocate a certain portion of the value of the enterprise to the Muztazefin or the underprivileged. Given that many of these industries have other problems, ranging from labor-related issues to the lack of management skills to difficulty in obtaining spare parts and raw materials, this added burden was another discouragement to the private sector. As a result, the fate of these now state-owned industries remains unclear. As noted, some have suggested that the state return them to their original owners if the owners were not too closely identified with the shah's regime. With Iran's acute need for capital, the more moderate elements seem to be willing to lure back Iran's leading industrialists of the shah's period.

But the fate of these industries, and the fate of the private sector in general, depends on the outcome of political debate and on the Rafsanjani administration's ability to have its way and gain the confidence of the business community. By the end of 1991, however, prospects for the privatization of the Iranian economy looked brighter. In a November address to representatives from 128 developing countries gathered in Tehran to forge a common position in advance of the eighth United Nations Conference on Trade and Development, President Rafsanjani said that Iran will remove government controls on investment and production, deregulate banking and foreign trade, open a stock exchange, and vastly expand private ownership. The administration's efforts to gain the business community's confidence should benefit from a gradual but steady restoration of law and order. The breakthrough in peace with Iraq in the fall of 1990, which led to the withdrawal of Iraqi troops from Iranian territory, dramatically reduced the danger of war and boosted the morale and confidence of Iranian investors. In fact, according to the deputy governor of Iran's central bank, the private sector invested $66 million during 1989–1990.

Larger imports of consumer products and the revitalization of industry were also designed to ease another of the government's headaches – namely, the high rate of inflation. The government managed to drastically reduce its budget deficit and, hence, its domestic borrowing. According to the central bank's statistics, the inflation rate dropped from 28 percent in 1988–1989 to 17.5 percent in 1989–1990. In his New Year's message to the Iranian people on March 21, 1991, President Rafsanjani stated that the inflation rate for 1990–1991 was reduced to 8 percent. Despite some increase in production, however, Iran's economy did not experience the growth rates necessary for such a dramatic reduction. According to official statistics, the economy grew only 2 percent in the year ending March 1990. The economy performed much better in the 1990–1991 period, however, thanks to increased oil income and record imports valued at $22 billion. According to the IMF during this period, the economy grew at 10.5 percent. The estimated growth rate for 1991–1992 is about 8 percent. Although the measures noted above must have affected the inflation rate, the official rate has always been viewed as not reflecting the real magnitude of the problem.

Bringing some order into the exchange-rate situation and closing the gap between the official and black-market rates were other Rafsanjani priorities. Indeed, it was reported that Iran's minister of finance believed that the entire success of the government's economic policy depended on rectifying the anomalous exchange rate.

The Rafsanjani administration first attacked this issue with great enthusiasm, vowing to stabilize the situation by October 1989. Part of its strategy was to offer foreign exchange at a competitive rate to industrial units to help them raise production. These rates were initially to float with the aim of improving control of the free market. But after one adjustment, the competitive rate was first established at a ratio of $1 to RLS 800 and then reduced to a ratio of $1 to RLS 600. This policy has not been as successful as was hoped, however, partly because such a policy requires massive and long-term intervention by the central bank, a situation that Iran's shortages of foreign exchange do not allow. In fact, the competitive exchange rate has not so far been supplied in the quantities needed or quickly enough. Another measure the government adopted to regularize the exchange rate was its legalization of free-market foreign exchange dealers. As a result, Iran has a three-tier foreign exchange system. In practice, most of the nonofficial transactions are done according to the free market rate, which has been steady in the past two years at about $1 = IR 1400.

In addition to economic factors, Iran's foreign exchange problem has political roots. It is not likely, therefore, to be completely resolved before some of these problems are eliminated. One problem, the uncertainty over the issue of peace with Iraq, has been removed. In fact, as soon as the news of Iraq's acceptance of Iran's peace conditions surfaced in August 1990 and Iraqi troops began to withdraw from Iran, the black-market rate of the rial against the dollar grew stronger.

As law and order improve and the economy picks up, business confidence and private investment should increase. These developments would direct most of the available liquidity into productive investment, away from currency speculation, thus narrowing the gap between the official and black-market rate. Ultimately, when other conditions permit – especially the inflationary pressures – the rial will have to be devalued to get a rate that reflects Iran's real economic conditions.

In fact, a devaluation of the rial was discussed in Iran, as was the idea of a new currency called "noor." But because of concern over their negative economic and political fall-outs, both ideas have been shelved. A devaluation would exacerbate inflationary pressures and widen the income distribution gap. In particular, it would worsen the situation of fixed-income segments of the society. Nevertheless, an eventual devaluation at around the current competitive rate is expected as soon as domestic production has increased. The latest indication from the government is that as soon as the dollar falls close to IR 1000, the central bank will officially devalue the rial. Meanwhile, the government is envisaging salary increases and other measures to cushion the inflationary impact of devaluation on the most vulnerable segments of society.[57]

The Five-Year Development Plan

The Rafsanjani administration's long-term challenge was to come up with a realistic framework for Iran's development, work out the means of financing it, and get parliament to approve the plan.

The administration's ability to get its plan through the parliament was, furthermore, viewed as a test of President Rafsanjani's political clout and an indication of his ability to steer the country in the right direction despite the problems created by an occasionally truculent parliament. The Rafsanjani administration passed this test.

The plan the Rafsanjani administration proposed to the parliament was a very heavily revised version of an earlier plan prepared by the cabinet of Prime Minister Hossein Moussavi. The plan had to be revised not only because of new economic considerations and differences in economic philosophy between ex-Prime Minister Moussavi and President Rafsanjani, but also because dramatic events in the Soviet Union and Eastern Europe had changed the international political scene.

The Moussavi government, because of its ideological inclination, had relied heavily on cooperation with the Soviet Union, East European countries, China, and North Korea. With the changes in the USSR, the whole basis of his development strategy became unstuck. While Iran still has plans for cooperating with the Soviets, it is clear that it has to look elsewhere for capital and technology.

The original Moussavi plan projected an annual growth rate of 5 percent. The oil revenues during the lifetime of the plan were estimated at $63 billion. At the completion of the plan, it was expected that 2 million new jobs would have been created. Some foreign financing to obtain the foreign exchange required by the plan was sanctioned by Ayatollah Khomeini himself. The plan also envisaged reducing the inflation rate to around 11 percent by the end of the plan in 1993.

Many of these targets have been raised in the Rafsanjani administration's plan. The total cost of the plan is estimated to be $394 billion, with a hard currency component of $119 billion. The government projects its hard currency earnings from oil and gas during the plan to be $83 billion. Another $9 billion is expected from non-oil exports, bringing the total estimated foreign exchange earnings to $92 billion. This means Iran will have to raise $27 billion in foreign credits. Raising this amount will not be easy, given the domestic political constraints and the unwillingness of the Western governments and the international institutions to lend much to Iran without some concessions by Iran on foreign policy.

Iran's financial prospects have improved as a result of the Persian Gulf crisis and an increase in oil prices. Because of the need to enlist Iran's cooperation in the embargo against Iraq, some Western countries and Japan have been more forthcoming in raising capital for certain industrial projects.[58] For a long-term improvement in Iran's financial outlook, however, the price of oil should remain firm for a sustained time, not just experience periodic, short-lived increases prompted by political crises.

Another obstacle to a successful implementation of the plan – and one the authorities themselves have admitted – derives from bureaucratic inefficiencies and the shortages of technical and managerial expertise. In fact, in an interview with the Tehran Radio, Morteza Alviri, chairman of the Iranian Parliament's Planning and Budget Commission, conceded that "if the executive machinery of the nation stays the same as it is now, it will certainly not be able to implement the five-year plan, and the plan will fail."[59]

The Rafsanjani administration has taken measures to reform and streamline the bureaucracy. The question is how extensive and effective these reforms will be and how rapidly they will be carried out.

On the macroeconomic level, the plan's objectives are to increase investment and production and, consequently, the overall GNP. The annual overall growth of the GNP is projected at 8 percent. The growth rate, however, varies for different sectors. Agriculture is supposed to grow by 6.1 percent; oil, 8.7 percent; industry, 14.2 percent; mining, 19.5 percent; water, gas, and electricity, 9.1 percent; construction, 14.5 percent; and services, 6.2 percent. During the first year of the Rafsanjani administration, however, the economy grew only 2 percent. Given that in the last several years Iran has had a negative growth rate, this figure is quite encouraging, but it falls short of what is needed. As noted, however, prospects for growth have greatly improved; barring political problems or a sudden drop in oil prices, the government should be able to achieve the plan's target. During the plan's lifetime, the per capita income is projected to increase at an average annual rate of 4.8 percent. Investment is projected to grow at 11.6 percent annually. The government hopes to create 394,000 new jobs each year, thereby reducing the unemployment rate to 14 percent.

By increasing investment and production and by reducing the budget deficit, the government hopes to bring the rate of inflation down to 8.9 percent by 1993.

Whether the plan can meet these goals will also depend on the government's ability to curb the population increase. The government hopes to reduce the annual rate of population growth to 2.9 percent by the end of the plan.

Sectoral priorities of the plan include the expansion of the oil and gas sector, industry, and mining; the expansion of the country's communication network, including rail and air; the expansion and improvement of ports and airports; and an emphasis on primary and intermediate industry, rather than consumer industry. The growth of the industrial section is divided in the following way: primary industries, 24 percent; intermediary, 20 percent; and consumer, 4.2 percent.[60]

The plan's hard currency needs are estimated to be $127 billion. The bulk of the hard currency will come from the sale of oil and gas. The plan estimates that Iran's oil exports will increase from 1.482 million barrels per day (mb/d) in 1367 (1989–1990) to 2.23 mb/d in 1373 (1995–1996). Since the ratification of the plan, the government has raised its projection of Iran's oil production and export capacity. According to a statement made by Iran's minister of oil in October 1991, Iran's oil production would reach 4.5 mb/d by March 1993. Given Iran's domestic consumption of about 1 mb/d, this would mean an increase in exports of more than 1 mb/d. Iran's drive to increase its production capacity is largely determined by the expectation that future OPEC quotas would be decided on the basis of production as favored by Saudia Arabia, which has the most flexible production capacity among OPEC members. The plan estimates that the price of oil will increase from $14.2 per barrel in 1990 to $21.4 in 1996. This estimate, however, was made before the Persian Gulf crisis, when the price of oil at several points passed the $30 mark. This increase in oil prices since August 1990 has provided Iran with close to $3 billion in windfall profits. It is not clear what the ultimate impact of the crisis will be on oil prices. But the earlier expectation that the decade of the 1990s would bring a steady rise in oil prices is not likely to materialize. Indeed, some foresee a possible oil glut and downward pressure on prices as Persian Gulf states increase their production to meet war-related and reconstruction expenditures.

Another unknown in the oil picture is the future of Soviet oil production and export. If expected investments to renovate the Soviet oil industry do not materialize and the level of Soviet oil production and export diminishes, upward pressure on oil prices would increase. The plan estimates the oil revenues, including the advanced sale of oil, at around $81.465 million, plus $1.640 million from the sale of gas. Another $17.830 million is expected to come from non-oil exports. This may be too optimistic a figure, however. Other estimates have put the non-oil revenues at $9.500 million. Of the total foreign exchange earnings, nearly $10 billion will be spent on defense. This leaves a foreign exchange gap of $27 billion, which surely must be adjusted upward in light of the damage done by the earthquake and the increased need for imports. Of $27 billion, $10 billion will be spent on reviving existing industries, and $9 billion on new industrial, mining, and agricultural projects. The $10 billion will be raised through buy-back schemes whereby factories import primary materials and repay the cost through earnings from the export of finished products. Iran's ability to raise the foreign financing needed for the completion of the plant, however, depends heavily on its ability to improve its international ties, particularly with the West.

During 1990–1991, there were some encouraging trends in this direction—particularly, several visits by World Bank and IMF experts to Iran.[61] Although Iran has said it does not want to borrow from the IMF, resumption of these contacts and the relatively positive reaction of the visiting team could help Iran to raise financing. The World Bank itself will grant Iran an emergency loan for the reconstruction of earthquake-damaged areas. A group of French bankers has also raised $1.5 million for a number of petrochemical projects.[62] The outlook for more French and other

European, as well as Japanese and Canadian, financing improved further in 1991.

Some of Iran's most important development projects, either under way or planned, are as follow.

Oil and Gas

The government intends to raise the country's annual petrochemical output from the current level of 3 million metric tons to 8 million metric tons by 1995. To achieve this goal, the government is planning to build a large petrochemical complex in Tabriz in northwestern Iran, to complete the huge petrochemical complex in Arak (central Iran), and to repair the war-damaged petrochemical complex at Bandar Khomeini. Other plans are envisaged for the petrochemical complexes in Isfahan and Abadan, for Mashhad in the northeast, and along the Caspian Sea coast.

Work has begun on a $1 billion gas refinery at Nar-Kangan, and another refinery is planned for Aghar-Dalan, northeast of the Nar-Kargan. Other plans involve the Sarkhun fields near Bandar Abbas in the south and the Sarakhs fields near the Afghan and Soviet borders. The government is planning to expand the domestic network of gas distribution both for domestic consumption and industrial use to reduce dependence on oil-product import and to save more oil for export.[63]

Industry and Mining

Along with industrial expansion and the effective exploitation and utilization of the country's mineral resources, power generation is one of the nation's top priorities. According to some estimates, Iran will need 4,000 additional megawatts (MW) in the next few years to keep pace with demand. The priority in this regard is on repairing the war-damaged plants and completing the half-built ones. In fact, in presenting its budget for the Iranian year 1370 (March 21, 1991–1992), the government has said that power generation will be increased by 790 MW, to bring the total capacity to 15,000 MW. This would enable the government to bring electricity to 2,000 additional villages, raising the number of villages having electricity to 27,000.

Increasing steel production is another priority. The government wants to increase the total steel output to 6 million metric tons by the early 1990s. This will be done by expanding the capacity of Soviet-built mills in Isfahan, rebuilding the Ahwaz complex, completing the Mobarakeh complex in Isfahan, and building a new plant in the Qishm Island. Japan is a major participant in these projects. Italy is involved in the building of the Mobarakeh complex, the first stage of which was completed in 1991.

In addition, the capacity of the Arak aluminum plant will be expanded, and a new plant will be set up in Bandar Abbas in the south. The annual capacity of the Sarcheshmeh copper complex is to be raised to 145,000 metric tons, and a new copper products plant is being set up. Automotive industries have also been given priority, and cooperation with French, Italian, and British companies is encouraged. Recently, Iran and the French carmaker Peugeot reached a 10-year agreement to produce cars, buses, minibuses, and vans. Negotiations are also under way with Renault and Italy's Fiat. Negotiations with Fiat have included the production of trucks, tractors, road-building machinery, and passenger cars. Cement, sugar, and paper products are other favored areas of industrial activity. Brazil and Finland are favored partners in the latter two ventures.[64]

Transport

The expansion and upgrading of the country's road and transport network is another priority. During the life of the five-year plan, the government hopes to build 11 new airports, including the giant Haft-e-Tir International Airport for Tehran, and to renovate 31 existing airports; expand the railway network by 550 kilometers and complete the 1,000 kilometers of existing lines; build 359 kilometers of highways, 1,397 kilometers of main roads, and 1,530 kilometers of secondary roads. In addition, urban railways are planned for Tehran and all cities with populations of more than 500,000 such as Tabriz and Mashhad.[65]

Agriculture

The increase in the output of major crops and mechanization of irrigated farming are among the government's agricultural priorities. Among the more ambitious plans for agricultural development is one in the north to improve rice yield and to teach the peasants modern farming and irrigation techniques. This project will be implemented with help from the Japan International Cooperation Agency. Another plan is a large agro-industrial complex in Khusistan in the south.[66]

4

Culture and Society: Toward a
New Islamo-Nationalist Synthesis?

When it came to power, the Islamic regime was determined to eliminate all elements of the Iranian culture it viewed as counter to Islamic principles or as a threat to Islam's preeminent role in Iran. This meant reversing the secularizing policies of the Pahlavi era in the educational and judicial systems; imposing a strict moral code on the population, enforced by special squads; and trying to eliminate traces of Iran's pre-Islamic culture and the influence of Persian nationalism.

In addition to Islamizing Iran's cultural life, the regime tried to instill a revolutionary spirit into the country's cultural and artistic life. Indeed, a principal tenet of the Islamic regime's cultural philosophy was that "art must be at the service of Islam and the revolution." In other words, artistic expression had merit only insofar as it advanced the goals of the revolution (i.e., by instilling an Islamic and revolutionary spirit in the people). By contrast, all forms of art that encouraged a decadent, anti-Islamic, and antirevolutionary spirit were prohibited.

Many of these principles still determine the Islamic regime's attitude toward cultural issues. But during the last 10 years, and especially in the last few years, subtle but significant changes have occurred in the government's attitude toward cultural issues, especially as far as the "Iranian" dimension of the country's culture is concerned.

Strongly negative reactions to certain aspects of the cultural policy spurred most of these changes, as the regime came to realize that excessive anti-Iranianism would damage its base of support among the Iranians.

Moreover, once in power, the Islamists no longer felt seriously threatened by Iranian nationalism as an ideological rival. As a result, the religious establishment began reverting to its more traditional attitude toward Iran's pre-Islamic culture and its relationship to Islam, as well as to the post-Islamic Iranian culture, with its delicate blending of Islamic principles, pre-Islamic Persian concepts, and other non-Islamic philosophies.

This attitude could be summed up as follows. True, all pre-Islamic societies were living in ignorance and darkness ("Jaheliya"), and the Persian empire was no exception. Even during this era of darkness, however, the Persians were better than other peoples, and their society was better than other societies.

One sign of the superiority of pre-Islamic Iranian society is the ease with which the Iranians accepted Islam. In this regard, the role played by Salman the Persian (also known as Salman the Pure One) as one of Prophet Mohammad's earliest companions is emphasized. Indeed, as noted earlier, many prominent clerical figures in the past had produced "Hadith" from the Shi'a Imams about the Iranians' special place and role in the Islamic community.

In addition, the religious establishment has been aware of Iran's vast contributions to the development of Islamic culture and to the spread of Islam in such far-off places as India, Southeast Asia, China, and even parts of Africa.[67] In the last few years, the Islamic regime has also begun to revert to this traditional position.

In addition to the popular reaction, two other factors have helped the Islamists return to a more traditional position about the mix of Islam and Iranianism in Iran's cultural identity. One of these factors was external: the Iraqi invasion of Iran. To rally popular support for the war effort, the government had to appeal not only to Islam, but also to Iranian nationalism.

The Iraqi propaganda depicting Iranians as the "fire-worshiping Persians," while the Iranian government was trying to emphasize Islamic brotherhood and encourage the use of Arabic in Iran, enhanced the Iranians' sense of their cultural distinctiveness.

The other factor was the more utilitarian considerations of influence and material gain. Many in the regime became aware that undermining the Persian language and culture was not helping them compete for the leadership of the Muslim world and was also detrimental to Iran's prestige in the community of nations.[68]

The regime also came to realize that Iran's historic and cultural legacy was an asset that could have material payoffs. This realization came about when the government began to consider reviving the country's tourism industry. The five-year development plan specifically provides for conserving and restoring Iran's historic monuments and for encouraging international tourism. Even the Ayatollah Khamenei called the ruins of Iran's ancient capital of Takht-e-jamshid (Persepolis) a heritage of mankind that must be preserved. President Rafsanjani went one step further when he visited Persepolis in April 1991 and called on the Iranians "to reinforce their national dignity." Only a few years earlier, they had been called the legacy of corrupt monarchies, which should be destroyed.

This gradual change has had significant practical consequences for the Islamic regime's attitude toward the Iranian dimension of the country's identity and culture and its cultural policy. The following are the most important of these consequences.

Relegitimizing Iranianism

The most important change for the Islamic regime has been to accept and legitimize the concept of Iran and Iranianism as a coequal focus with Islam of national loyalty and a component of Iranian cultural identity. The regime has now accepted the notion of an "Iranian nation," and it has also concluded that the nature of the Iranian culture is "Iranian Islamic." This may at first appear to be a minor change, until one remembers that at the beginning of the revolution, the new regime did everything in the name of Islam and the Umat-al-Islam, a much more broader concept. Of course, even now, the Islamic element is emphasized more. But the trend is toward accepting the mutual dependence and inter-penetration of Iran and Iranian Islam, and realizing that one without the other would be much poorer culturally and spiritually and would not represent the true feelings of the people.

Rehabilitating Iran's Literary Figures

One element of this reemergence of Iranianism has been the rehabilitation of leading Iranian literary figures whose poetry and works had been banned. A manifestation of this process was the convening of an international conference on the one-thousandth anniversary of Hafiz Shirazi's birth, Hafiz is arguably Iran's — and even the Muslim world's — greatest mystic and poet. Convening such a conference was of considerable significance because Hafiz's poetry is full of love, wine, and doe-eyed houris — albeit in allegorical terms — as well as criticism of the hypocritical and corrupt clergy and ostentatiously pious people.

But the most significant event in this literary rehabili-tation was the publication of the Ayatollah Khomeini's own mystical poems addressing themes similar to those of Hafiz and other great Persian mystics. There are still, however, exceptions — for example, Omar Khayyam's work, which has still not been rehabilitated.

Encouraging the Arts, Publishing, and Electronic Media

The regime's approach to several issues related to artistic expression has become more relaxed. One such area is mu-sic, which got a new lease on life after the Ayatollah Kho-

meini authorized the buying and selling of musical instruments, provided they were not used for corrupt purposes.
As a result, classical Persian music and the more nationalist type of singing have improved in quality. In the last few
years, there have even been occasional performances of classical Western music. Rhythmic music with a strong beat,
whether Persian or Western, however, is still not permitted.

Since the revolution and because of it, the art of the
poster has flourished in Iran. The government has also encouraged the art of calligraphy. Despite Islam's prohibition
of portrait painting, painting that has traditionally been a
strong component of pre- and post-Islamic Persian culture
has not suffered in Iran. In fact, a form of it has expanded.
Painting is taught at both government and private schools,
and regular exhibitions are held in Tehran and other big
cities. In 1986, an exhibition of West German painters was
held at the Contemporary Arts Museum in Tehran. Photog-
raphy also has been encouraged, and some Iranian photog-
raphers have won awards abroad.

But more than any other art form, the film industry has
expanded in Iran. The quality of films has also improved, in
the sense that they treat more serious subjects; in the past,
they mostly consisted of low-quality comedies or musicals
similar to films produced on the Indian subcontinent. The
filmmakers do not have sufficient freedom, however; they
are restrained both by political considerations and by the
imperatives of Islamic morality. Nevertheless, in the last
few years the government's attitude in both respects has
relaxed. Likewise, the government has liberalized its attitude in regard to importing quality foreign films, and it
encourages contact between the Iranian filmmakers and
those around the world. The most important vehicle for
such contact is the Fajr International Film Festival, held
annually in Tehran. In addition, Iranian filmmakers participate in international film festivals.

Theater has also been encouraged, with particular emphasis on staging plays by Iranian playwriters, mostly with
war-related or other social issues. In the last few years,

there has been a revival of the works of non-Iranian play-wrights, including such Western masters of tragedy and comedy as Shakespeare and Moliere. A theatre festival is held with the Fajr International Film Festival.

Despite shortages of paper and other printing material, more books have been published in the country, as well as many dailies and periodicals. In addition, radio and television have cultural and artistic programs. Iran has two radio and television networks. The first network's programs cover 90 percent of the country and the second network 65 percent.

The government has paid a great deal of attention to expanding the electronic communications network, partly for political and ideological reasons (i.e., to spread its ideology and influence among the masses). Whatever the government's motives, this development will enhance the people's social and political consciousness. Under the right circumstances, it could help develop broad-based national social and political institutions.

In short, Iran is not the cultural wasteland it is often considered in the West. In some respects, the reduction in Western cultural influence and the emphasis on so-called cultural independence has revitalized Iran's indigenous culture. This is true of classical Persian music, for example, which was losing its purity.

Ideological and political restrictions, however, have severely limited Iran's cultural scene. Some of the developments referred to earlier, especially a gradual but steady rehabilitation of Iranianism and relative flexibility, have improved the environment for Iran's cultural life. But both trends must continue and be enhanced before Iran can experience a true and indigenous cultural and artistic renaissance.

Because culture and politics are closely related, especially in a country like Iran with two strong poles of identity — Islam and Iranian nationalism — the evolution of Iran's political debate and its outcome will determine how Iran's cultural scene evolves. The course with the greatest potential for both Iran's national unity and its cultural renaissance would be to reconcile Iran's nationalist and Islamic heritages, as it had always been before the polarization of the last century, especially during the Pahlavi years.

Islamization of Education: Challenges of Modernity

One of the first steps taken by the Islamic regime as part of its overall cultural revolution was the reform of the educational system.[69] This process has had many dimensions, from changing the textbooks to making the knowledge of Islamic rules an indispensable requirement for being accepted into university.

The principal reason for this reform was political—namely, to educate the present and future generations in the ideology of the state. The same policy was adopted by the Pahlavis, who tried to embrace and instill an Iranian nationalist spirit into the people because that was the state ideology. History books of the Pahlavi period, for example, often emphasized Iran's pre-Islamic past and the role of its great kings. The reverse has been the case under the new regime. The second goal of the reform, at least initially, was to combat the culture of consumerism and fascination with the West.

As in China's cultural revolution, the Islamic cultural revolution has damaged the quality of education in Iran. This is not, however, because of Islam. Indeed, after Islamization, Iran experienced a scientific and literary renaissance. The Iranian viziers of both its Arab and Turkic rulers (such as the Bermakis, who literally ran the Abbasid Khalifat in Baghdad, and Nezam al-Molk, the vizier of the Turkic Seljuks) created great centers of Islamic learning such as the Nezamiyeh School of Baghdad. Indeed, the egalitarian dimensions of Islam, as opposed to the caste system of the Sassanids, made it possible for Iranians of low birth to excel in the sciences and the arts.

The problem after the Islamic revolution involved according priority to revolutionary zeal rather than to academic excellence in choosing the students and teachers and the lack of tolerance for open debate and intellectual freedom.

The exodus of many intellectuals and experts has harmed Iran's educational system. Other problems have also undermined an educational system that, even before the revolution, was inadequate for the country's needs and of poor quality.

These problems derive from the lack of money and trained personnel and a rapid rate of population growth. The following figures indicate the magnitude of the task facing Iran in providing educational facilities for its people. Between 1980 and 1988, 27,500 new schools with 115,000 classes have been constructed, mostly in rural areas. But government officials estimate that as many schools should be built in less than half that time to meet the needs of 1 million new students who reach school age every year.

Another serious problem is the lack of enough good teaching staff. The dearth of good teachers is partly the result of the fact that the teaching profession, particularly for primary schools, is not very popular. For example, the teacher training colleges can accept up to 22,000 applicants annually, but the number of applicants falls short. Moreover, those who do go to teachers' training schools are high school graduates with poor grades who make poor teachers.

Lack of qualified candidates bedevils higher education. In the year 1987–1988, for example, only 65,000 of 667,000 applicants were admitted to higher education. In 1989–1990, the number of applicants reached 752,343, only 61,000 of whom were admitted. As noted, in choosing the applicants, academic excellence is not the only or even the most important criterion. Rather, priority has been given to those who volunteered to serve in the war with Iraq and those with a better knowledge of Islamic rules. Facilities for higher education, such as laboratories, are also stretched thin.

The government is aware of these problems and the negative consequences a poor educational system has on the country's economic and technological recovery and progress. Thus, President Rafsanjani, immediately after assuming power as Iran's chief executive, emphasized the necessity of cultural and educational revitalization for Iran's future in his speech presenting his cabinet to the parliament. He particularly made the point that academic excellence should be the principal criterion for gaining access to education and jobs. Such statements are more easily made in speeches than realized, as their implementation would go against entrenched material interests of various powerful groups.

Research and Development

The Iranian government's efforts to gain technological self-sufficiency have included encouraging indigenous research and development (R&D). The responsibility to oversee R&D programs in the country lies with the National Research Council. The Industrial and Scientific Research Organization is the principal research organization for the government.

In the last few years, a variety of research institutes and organizations have been set up. It is very difficult, however, to assess the amount and quality of work done in these organizations.

What is clear is that, for a serious research effort in the coming years, the government will need to spend more funds and liberalize the political and intellectual atmosphere. The latter is particularly important in social sciences. Without liberalization, Iran's problems of brain drain will continue as its best minds go unused and its best talent leaves the country.

5

Foreign Relations: Continuity and Change

Certain fundamental factors that have deeply affected Iran's approach toward the outside world should be noted before explaining the state of Iran's foreign relations at the time of the revolution. Their influence was felt even by the Islamic republic despite its more ideological approach to the conduct of foreign affairs. In part, the regime was forced to bend its ideology in response to these influences. Paramount among these factors is Iran's geopolitical position. This position not only has made Iran an arena of great power rivalry in the last 200 years, it has also rendered it extremely vulnerable to events beyond its control, especially changes in the great power relations and the character of regional and international political systems.[70]

The second most important factor is Iran's historical experience both as a great culture and empire and as a declining country subject to great power manipulation, resulting in territorial losses and national humiliation. Both experiences have affected Iran's self-image and the Iranians' perceptions of their position in the outside world and their national aspirations. The influence of Iran's historical experience has been felt by all Iranians of varying political and ideological views, including the Islamists of the 1979 revolution.[71]

The third and fourth important factors affecting Iran's relation with the outside world in the last 200 years have been its military, economic, and technological weakness and its quest for modernization.

These last two factors have both limited Iran's foreign policy options and have necessitated adapting Iran's foreign policy to its economic and technological needs. Indeed, as will be discussed later, these two factors have forced the Islamic regime to curb its ideological excesses and adopt a more pragmatic foreign policy. In the future as well, these factors will affect Iran's foreign policy considerably.

Iran's Foreign Relations in 1979

By the time of the Islamic revolution, the cornerstone of Iran's foreign policy was its strategic, political, and economic alliance with the West, especially the United States.

Iran's relations with the Soviet Union had stabilized along reasonable lines, and bilateral economic relations between the two countries had expanded. A direct Soviet threat to Iran's security, whether in the form of military incursion or active subversion, had diminished. Nevertheless, the Soviet Union's ultimate objective vis-à-vis Iran—namely, to make it a client state—had not changed. Thus, the Soviet Union in a sense was still Iran's number one security problem. Soviet policy toward Iran since the mid-1960s was conducted on two levels. Government to government, the Soviets tried to normalize political relations, easing tension and expanding economic ties that were highly profitable to them. At another level, however, the Soviets tried to encircle Iran with pro-Soviet governments through their activities in Iraq, the Persian Gulf/Arabian peninsula region, and the Indian subcontinent and through support both to radical Arab forces that were viciously anti-Iranian and to leftist and religious opposition to the shah.

Because of these Soviet policies, the shah used to talk of a Soviet pincer pressure on Iran.[72] The Soviets, for their

part, were particularly concerned and angry about the
shah's policies in Afghanistan and the Indian subcontinent.
These policies were aimed largely at weakening Afghan and
Indian ties to the Soviet Union by offering them economic
and other incentives that the oil revolution of 1973 made
possible.[73]

Nor were Iranian efforts to counter radical and pro-
Soviet tendencies limited to these areas; they extended to
the Middle East and Africa.[74] Indeed, all through the
1970s, Iran's foreign policy had become very activist, and
its geographic range had dramatically expanded.

Iran was first propelled into playing an important regional role by the 1968 British decision to withdraw militarily from the Persian Gulf. At the time, this British decision
created a serious power vacuum in the region; the United
States, mired in the Vietnam conflict, was neither willing
nor able to take Britain's place.

Neither alone nor collectively did any of the emerging
Persian Gulf Arab states have the military or human resources to perform Britain's traditional security role. Iran,
therefore, was chosen as the principal instrument of Western security policy in the Persian Gulf. It became the first
test of the new U.S. strategy, enunciated in the Nixon doctrine, of using regional powers to perform security tasks on
behalf of the West.

The shah accepted the challenge enthusiastically. Moreover, he later went beyond the task assigned to him and
developed the ambition of turning Iran into an Indian
Ocean power. The oil revolution of 1973 and the ensuing
dramatic improvement in Iran's financial position made this
goal appear within reach. The excessive zeal with which
Iran under the shah performed this security task and the
increasing activism and the expanding range of Iran's foreign policy interests proved very costly, both domestically
and internationally.

Domestically, many people resented the cost of this activist foreign policy, particularly the buildup of Iran's military forces. The popular feeling was that the funds spent on

the military buildup, foreign aid, and so on should be used for economic development and improvement in the people's living standards.[75] Moreover, many Iranians felt that Iran was serving Western interests rather than Iran's national interests. They felt that Iran's overactivist policy was antagonizing many of its neighbors and thus damaging its interests.

Iran's activist role was also resented by regional countries, particularly the Arab states. The radical Arabs, who had always resented Iran's role as a pro-Western country with close ties—albeit informal—to Israel, looked with an especially hostile eye at this new Iranian role. In fact, Iranian activism brought intensified subversion by radical Arabs against the shah's regime.[76] Ironically, by the mid-1970s, Iran's policy on the Arab-Israeli issue had moved in a more pro-Arab direction and caused second thoughts and some concern in Israel about Iran and its growing regional role.

To finance its ambitious security and foreign policy goals, Iran adopted a militant position within the Organization of Petroleum Exporting Countries (OPEC) in regard to oil prices. Iran also increasingly assumed a hard-line posture on many economic issues of concern to the Third World in the context of the UN negotiations on a new international economic order. In a sadly ironic manner, however, Iran's championship of Third World goals did not do much to improve its image, that of a Western surrogate, among Third World states. Iran's negative image among many Third World countries—especially in Africa—sprang from its ties with South Africa and Israel. In addition, pro-Soviet and other radical Third World states disliked Iran's pro-Western tendencies.

Meanwhile, these aspects of Iran's foreign policy, plus the shah's arrogant personal style, created tensions in Iran's relations with its Western allies. Many in the West began to see Iran as more of a nuisance than an asset. It should be noted that by the time of the Iranian revolution and the year preceding it, East-West détente, while moribund, was not dead, and the Soviets had not yet invaded Afghanistan. Moreover, the Persian Gulf Arab states, awash in oil money, had survived their birth pangs and appeared more stable and confident.

As a result, there was a growing feeling that the West no longer needed Iran as much as it did in the late 1960s and early 1970s. This train of thought was reflected in growing criticism in the West, particularly in the U.S. Congress, of Iran's military buildup and human rights abuses. President Jimmy Carter's administration, which assumed office in 1977, in particular seemed to favor fundamental changes in Iran. In short, by the time of the revolution, Iran's foreign policy orientation and its overactivism were resented at home and created serious tensions in its relations with both its allies and its enemies.

Before discussing the changes that the revolution introduced in Iran's foreign relations and the evolution of Iran's foreign policy after it, especially since the passing of the Ayatollah Khomeini, the following points on the ideological and cultural context of Iran's foreign policy before the revolution should be noted. This is very important because, as was the case with all aspects of Iran's collective life, the ideology of Islamic revolution profoundly affected the ideological and cultural context of Iran's relations with the outside world.

Similarly, the most important aspect of the evolution of Iran's foreign relations since the revolution has been the adaptation of this revolutionary ideology to both Iran's and the world's realities. The ideological and cultural framework of Iran's foreign policy before the revolution was nationalist and statist. Iran as a territorial and national expression was the sole focus of policy. The objective of its foreign policy was to achieve its collective interests as perceived and interpreted by the shah and the political elite associated with him. In other words, Iran's foreign policy was not principally concerned with achieving any universalist principles.

Within this nationally focused context, Iran nevertheless shared interests with two sets of countries in regard to two sets of issues. The first group was composed of the anti-Communist countries, both in the West and within the Third World. Under the shah, Iran saw its security and strategic interests to be linked to these countries. Of course, this did not mean total harmony, particularly in regional terms. For example, at least in the Persian Gulf, Iran aspired to leadership – a role the West did not view very favorably – even though in broad strategic terms, Western and Iranian security interests coincided on such issues as containing Soviet and other radical forces.

The second group was made up of Third World countries with whom Iran shared many interests, in particular the reform of international economic and financial systems. After the oil revolution of 1973, the ensuing severe financial difficulties for most Third World countries, and Iran's hawkish attitude on oil prices, the coincidence of interests vastly diminished.

Developments after the Revolution

The Islamic revolution changed Iran's foreign relations considerably. First and foremost, it enhanced the ideological and universalist – as opposed to statist and nationalist – dimensions of its foreign policy. Thus, the spread of revolutionary Islam became the primary objective of Iran's foreign policy – at least its stated goal. Similarly, safeguarding the interests of the Islamic community, rather than maximizing Iran's national interest, and creating what some have characterized as a new Islamic order became the declared objectives of foreign policy.

In practice, however, the Islamic regime had to adjust its foreign policy to the realities of other influences, most notably those of Iran's geopolitical situation, historical experience, and domestic and international constraints. Moreover, while the world view of the Islamic regime was principally influenced by Islam as interpreted by Ayatollah Ruhollah Khomeini, other influences, such as Iran's cultural and historical experiences, foreign ideologies, and political themes current in the Third World in the last several decades have also contributed to molding this view. In many respects, the ideological precepts of the new regime repeated Third World themes in Islamic terms using Islamic symbols.[77]

As was the case with issues pertaining to the country's economic, social, and political life, the leadership disagreed on the interpretation of Islamic principles as they applied to the conduct of Iran's foreign relations. Part of this intraregime disagreement resulted from the fact that some of the Islamic leaders and their secular allies were more influenced by socialist ideas—particularly Third World varieties.[78] This group was—and most of its members still are—viscerally anti-Western and especially anti-American. They favored having better ties with the Soviet Union, the Eastern bloc, and Third World countries. They favored actively exporting revolution, even if at times it meant recourse to subversion and terrorism.

The other group, by contrast, was more concerned about the Soviet/Communist threat from Iran's security. Thus, while by no means pro-Western, and certainly not pro-American, this faction favored maintaining some relations with the West as a counterweight to Soviet power and proximity. Although also committed to exporting the revolution, this group favored a more peaceful way of doing so, such as projecting the image of a successful and prosperous Islamic community.

It is important, however, to note that the urge to export the revolution did not derive solely from the Islamic dimensions of the new regime's ideology. Nor did it result solely from the proselytizing and expansionist tendencies inherent in any revolutionary ideology; indeed, secular leaders of the revolution also believed in the export of revolution. The question of the export of revolution had a security dimension. All states want to surround themselves with like-minded states in the belief that states sharing the same world view and perspective do not threaten each other's security. This practice is called creating a congenial security environment.[79]

Another significant trait of Iran's approach to foreign relations during the early years of revolution that differed markedly from Iran's approach before the revolution was the emphasis on so-called people-to-people rather than government-to-government relations. This, too, is a trait common to many revolutionary movements in the early stages of development. It derives from a naive faith in the superiority of the movements' ideas and the belief that they would be embraced by others if they could be adequately exposed to them. As has been the case with all other aspects of Iran's national life since the revolution, the conduct of Iran's postrevolution foreign policy has been deeply affected by its domestic politics.

Immediately after the revolution and during Prime Minister Mehdi Bazargan's transitional government, the competition was among three principal forces: Islamic nationalists, secular nationalists, and a variety of leftist groups. After the victory of Islamic forces, disagreements occurred within the Islamic leadership itself, as discussed earlier. These divisions, although less sharp than before, continue to affect foreign policy, as illustrated below.

The evolution of Iran's foreign policy since the revolution, however, can be explained best in terms of the gradual adjustment of a revolutionary movement to the internal realities of Iran itself and to the imperatives of living in a world and an interstate system that resists revolutionary efforts to upset its rules and equilibrium.

Iran's revolutionary leaders have also gone through a process of learning the rules of statecraft and conducting the affairs of a state and nation. In the process, most of them have developed from zealous revolutionaries into politicians and statesmen. This adjustment has accelerated and intensified since the passing of Ayatollah Khomeini, because Khomeini, though capable of pragmatism and realism, was perhaps the only true revolutionary within the Iranian leadership. Given his overwhelming influence, the impact of his personality was strongly felt in every aspect of Iranian life. The following is an analysis of the practical consequences of this learning and adjustment for Iran's foreign relations over the past 12 years.

The Transitional Period

Bazargan's Premiership
(February to November 1979)

Iran's foreign relations in this period — like all other aspects of its national life — had a dualistic and even chaotic aspect. The foreign policy philosophy of Prime Minister Bazargan's government was rooted in Iran's secular nationalist tradition, best exemplified by Dr. Mohammad Mossadegh. It was essentially a moderate version of a nonaligned philosophy. It was based on avoiding too much dependence on any one great power; staying clear of great power rivalries as much as possible; and maintaining good relations with all countries, especially neighboring states, through mutual respect and noninterference in each other's internal affairs.

Like most Iranian nationalists of both the secular and Islamic variety, however, Bazargan and his colleagues were apprehensive about the Soviet Union, given its proximity. They wanted to maintain good relations with the West to balance Soviet power.

The Bazargan government also advocated a less activist foreign policy than the one the shah pursued, especially in the Persian Gulf. Indeed, the Bazargan foreign policy in its essentials was not much different from the previous regime's under the premiership of Shahpour Bakhtiar. It was under Bakhtiar's premiership, for example, that Iran withdrew from Central Treaty Organization (CENTO) membership, severed its links with Israel and South Africa, and declared that it would no longer play the role of the Persian Gulf's gendarme.[80] While Bazargan was trying to pursue this moderate line, however, a variety of revolutionary groups was pursuing their own agenda of spreading the revolution. The activities of these groups caused difficulties in Iran's relations with other countries, especially its neighbors.

Both leftist and Islamic forces were opposed to Bazargan's policy of maintaining reasonable relations with the United States. Each, for its own reasons, wanted to eliminate rather than merely reduce the U.S. presence in Iran.

Occupying the U.S. embassy and holding U.S. diplomats and nationals hostage was the strategy these forces used to ensure an enduring enmity between Iran and the United States and thus eliminate the U.S. presence.[81]

Bani-Sadr Presidency

Although a coalition of Islamic, leftist, and what could best be described as opportunistic forces destroyed the Bazargan government, it took some time for Islamic forces to consolidate their power. For nearly 18 months, a number of personalities whose philosophy and outlook were influenced by both Islam and Iranian nationalism, such as Abol-Hassan Bani-Sadr and Sadegh Ghotbzadeh, exerted some influence on policy. Bani-Sadr was essentially an Iranian nationalist whose political philosophy was influenced by his clerical background and European—especially French—leftist and Third World thinking. Thus Bani-Sadr favored a more militant and activist type of nonaligned policy for Iran, especially in the service of Islamic causes.[82] Being very concerned about the Soviet threat, Bani-Sadr and Ghotbzadeh, too, wanted to maintain reasonable ties with the West. Ghotbzadeh in particular was almost virulently anti-Soviet.

Iran's foreign policy during this period was dominated by three issues: (1) The U.S. hostage crisis, (2) the internal power struggle, and (3) the Soviet invasion of Afghanistan. From November 4, 1979, until September 20, 1980, the U.S.

hostage crisis dominated both Iran's foreign policy and its domestic scene. The issue became inextricably linked with the power struggle among varying political forces and personalities.[83] The Soviet invasion of Afghanistan also caused deep anxiety in Iran. Yet given the depth of ideological and personal rivalries within Iran's revolutionary forces and the connection between these rivalries and the hostage crisis, even the Soviet invasion of Afghanistan did not prompt Iran to resolve the crisis until Iraq's invasion. The infighting, political chaos, and proliferation of revolutionary committees and organizations that characterized the Iranian scene during this period meant that Iran did not have a coherent foreign policy. Its foreign policy consisted of extreme anti-Americanism and an all-out call for Islamic revolution on the Iranian model throughout the Muslim world. Iran's revolutionary activities, however, were not conducted systematically and consisted mainly of rhetorical exhortations. As a result of this situation, Iran's interests and image were badly damaged. Iran's inflammatory rhetoric caused panic among its neighbors and their allies, and its excesses undermined the appeal of its ideology.

The long, drawn-out hostage crisis entailed heavy economic and political costs as Iran became the subject of a large-scale economic boycott and was branded an outlaw nation. Indeed, as will be discussed later, the legacy of the hostage crisis still prevents Iran's international rehabilitation and its reintegration into the community of nations.

After September 1980, the war with Iraq was Iran's principal preoccupation. But initially, even the war did not end the power struggle among various groups and personalities. In fact, because of these rivalries, Iran's defense against the invading Iraq suffered, allowing Iraq to advance deep into Iranian territory. It was only after the second round of political struggle in Iran ended with the ouster of Abol-Hassan Bani-Sadr from the presidency (and later his flight from Iran) and the victory of Islamic forces that Iran began to put up a credible defense against Iraq.

1981–1984: Radical Ascendancy
and the Export of Revolution

With the ouster of Bani-Sadr and later the imprisonment and execution of Sadegh Ghotbzadeh, Islamic forces scored a major victory. But the defeat of nationalist and Islamo-nationalist forces did not end Iran's power struggle. This struggle shifted to the left and continued within the Islamic leadership between the radical and the more moderate factions, as described earlier.

Among the leftist forces, the Islamo-Marxist Mujaheddin-e-Khalq were viewed as the most serious challenge to the Islamic forces and were dealt with first. This was followed by a crackdown on the secular left, such as the Fedayan-e-Khalq and a number of other small leftist parties. The oldest Communist movement in Iran, the Tudeh Party, however, was exempted from this crackdown, because it had decided to support the Islamic forces. Among its reasons was the belief that the Islamic revolution, which the Tudeh viewed as another basically bourgeois revolution, would not last long and would be followed by a truly socialist revolution.

Moreover, some of the radical elements within Islamic forces had had long-standing connections with the Tudeh Party; the Tudeh had chosen a strategy of infiltration from within and an eventual ouster of the more moderate elements.[84]

The Tudeh Party's strategy was also influenced by the Soviet Union's assessment of the nature of the Iranian revolution and the optimistic outlook for its transformation into a real socialist revolution.

The ascendancy of the radical elements within the Iranian leadership, plus the economic necessities of war and the effects of the Western embargo, led to a pro-Soviet tilt in Iran's foreign policy. This tilt never went so far as to undermine the basic principle of the postrevolution Iranian foreign policy symbolized by the slogan "Neither East Nor West." The imbalance in Iran's relations with the two super-

powers since the revolution has been more a function of
Iran's animosity toward the United States than its friend-
ship for the Soviet Union. Moreover, the Soviet-Iranian rap-
prochement during this period was also quite short lived.
By the summer of 1982, after Iran succeeded in forcing
Iraqi troops out of its territory, Soviet-Iranian relations became strained. This was largely because the Soviet assessment of the Iranian scene changed and because the Soviets
reevaluated their interests in light of developments both in
Iran and in the Middle East region.[85]

Changes in the balance of power within the Iranian
leadership and the erosion of the radicals' ascendancy contributed to the deterioration of Soviet-Iranian relations. In
April 1983, the Iranian government expelled 18 Soviet diplomats. This was followed by an extensive purge of leftist—
mostly Tudeh—and pro-Soviet elements from the Iranian
bureaucracy and the military. In addition, the Tudeh Party
was outlawed.

During this period, Iran's revolutionary and subversive
activities in the Arab world, especially in Lebanon, increased. In addition to the desire to export its revolution,
Iran's activities in the Arab world were aimed at undermining Western, especially U.S., interests and presence. This
aspect of Iran's policy was not only unsuccessful, but it also
entailed heavy costs to Iran by contributing greatly to a
dramatic shift in U.S. policy toward the Persian Gulf, the
Iran-Iraq War, and relations with Iraq.

The United States changed its policy from maintaining
a balance between Iran and Iraq in the war to actively sup-
porting Iraq. This change culminated in the U.S.-Iran confrontation of 1988. The United States also shifted from a
policy of containing Iran to one of punishing it. For a certain period, this desire to punish Iran was tempered by U.S.
fears of Iran's domination by the Soviet Union. But this
fear was eliminated after 1987 when Soviet policy changed
and U.S.-Soviet relations improved dramatically, leaving
the United States, free to pursue a punitive policy toward
Iran.

In this period, Iran's relations with West European countries also suffered to varying degrees, with Franco-Iranian relations suffering the most because of France's support for Iraq in the Iran-Iraq War and the Iranian-supported terrorist actions against French citizens in Lebanon. Meanwhile, relations with East European countries improved somewhat.

Overall, however, Iran's foreign relations and international standing suffered heavily. Yet, Iran's people-to-people diplomacy and its efforts to export its revolution did not succeed either. On the contrary, excesses of the Iranian revolutionaries, both at home and abroad, disillusioned many Muslims. The excesses also led to countermeasures by those countries that felt threatened by Iran's activities.

Perhaps the most devastating consequence of this behavior was the international community's attitude toward Iraq's aggression against Iran and its willingness not only to refuse to censor Iraq but to build it up by all necessary means.

1984–1988: Continued Tug of War, Fluctuation, and Creeping Realism

Iran's political scene during this period was characterized by the emergence of an uneasy balance between the moderate and radical wings of the Iranian leadership while competition for supremacy continued. This uneasy balance was periodically shifted in favor of one or the other group, with considerable implications for the country's foreign policy. These shifts were never decisive or long lasting, largely because of the Ayatollah Khomeini's unwillingness to support one group for any length of time and his insistence on keeping a balance between the two.

For Iranian foreign policy, this situation meant inconsistency, contradictory actions, and rapid and erratic changes; for Iran's partners, it meant uncertainty and confusion. In spite of such confusion, however, the revolutionary government of Iran was learning and adjusting to the international system and thus reexamining and revising some of the premises of its foreign policy.

The first sign of this process was Iran's realization that it could neither live outside the international community nor operate outside the interstate system. Of course, this realization was not equally shared by all elements within the leadership. The moderates were far more receptive to lessons derived from five years of revolutionary foreign policy and its disastrous consequences. A major breakthrough in the way Iran's foreign policy was conducted was a speech given by the Ayatollah Khomeini himself in October 1984 in which he stressed the necessity of having diplomatic relations with all countries. He said that the prophet of Islam considered it necessary to establish relations with other states. He excluded only Israel, the United States, and South Africa.

Other Iranian leaders, however, have said that if the United States changes its attitude toward the Islamic republic and the question of Palestine, U.S.-Iran ties could be reestablished. For the more pragmatic elements, a more conciliatory U.S. approach toward Iran itself would be enough, provided Iran's domestic politics permitted such a move.

In his speech, the Ayatollah Khomeini also attacked the proponents of the people-to-people approach to foreign relations. He characterized as irrational the view that "Iran must not have links with governments, but should establish links with people," and he insisted that lack of relations with other states ends in nothing but extinction and annihilation.

This speech inaugurated Iran's so-called open-door diplomacy. Iranian leaders, including then-President Hodjat-al-Islam Khamenei, Speaker of Parliament Hodjat-al-Islam Rafsanjani, and Foreign Minister Dr. Velayati, visited Japan, China, East Asia, Africa, and East and Southwest European countries between 1984 and 1988.

Iran's diplomatic offensive and the moderates' efforts to

reintegrate Iran into the international community were marred by the fact that their hold on decision making was not totally firm. Quite to the contrary, the radicals continued to put brakes on the normalization of Iran's foreign relations.

One of the radicals' tactics was to engage in terrorist activities abroad through official, semi-official, and nonofficial organizations that they either controlled or in which they wielded significant influence. The radicals were fully aware that these acts would bring negative reactions from the West and other countries, which they would then use to argue that the West was inherently against the Islamic regime and that the moderates' policy had no chance of success.

The other factor limiting Iran's flexibility in foreign policy was the continuation of the war with Iraq and Iran's inability either to win the war or to arrive at a negotiated peace. The regional politics of the Middle East, foreign policy objectives of the great powers, changes in the nature of great power relations, and domestic politics of Western countries also deeply affected their approach toward Iran, often limiting Iran's foreign policy choices and frustrating the moderates' efforts to normalize Iran's relations with the outside world.[86]

The regional politics of the Middle East affected the great powers, particularly the U.S. approach toward Iran. For example, some key U.S. Arab allies, such as Egypt and Saudi Arabia, did not favor improved U.S.-Iran relations because the U.S.-Iran confrontation enhanced their own value to the United States. They also believed U.S.-Iran hostility would prevent Iran from playing a significant regional role. During this period, Iran's foreign policy thus acquired a contradictory and dualistic nature. Its sharp fluctuations reflected the changing balance of power between the radical and moderate forces within the Iranian leadership.

Another turning point in Iran's thinking toward its foreign relations was the U.S. decision to reflag 11 Kuwaiti tankers in the spring of 1987, which led to a massive buildup of U.S. naval forces in the Persian Gulf and, finally, the military confrontation between the United States and Iran. In this confrontation, three Iranian warships and a number of offshore Iranian oil fields were destroyed or damaged.

The U.S. presence in the Persian Gulf helped Iraq in its war with Iran by undermining the Iranians' morale. Thus in April of 1988, Iraq, boosted by U.S. presence and with extensive use of chemical weapons, recaptured the Fao peninsula, which the Iranians had taken in 1986. Later, Iraq made other advances into Iranian territory.

These developments finally forced Iran to accept a negotiated peace based on UN Security Council Resolution 598. The history of the adoption of this resolution is in itself fascinating. Briefly, the resolution was part of the overall policy of pressure on Iran adopted by the United States and its Arab allies after the so-called Iran-contra fiasco of 1986–1987. Britain and the United States sponsored the resolution with the expectation that Iran would reject it, thereby enabling them to impose an arms embargo on Iran as provided for in the resolution.[87]

Iran did accept the resolution, however, with certain reservations. In fact, if the United States had been willing to be more flexible on a few points, there could have been a cease-fire earlier without major U.S.-Iran confrontation. With Iran weakened militarily and the Soviet threat drastically diminished, however, the United States was in no mood to accommodate Iran.

Nevertheless, Soviet and Chinese efforts within the United Nations to allow Iran more time to comply with the provisions of the resolution prevented the United States from imposing an arms embargo on Iran. Later, the Soviets would benefit from this behavior in terms of their relations with Iran.

Immediately following the cease-fire, there was a widespread questioning of past policies that reflected very negatively on the radicals, undermining their position and strengthening the hand of the moderates.

As a result, between Iran's acceptance of the cease-fire

in July 1988 and the outbreak of the Rushdie affair in February 1989, Iran pursued a policy of opening up toward the West and settling old differences. There was even speculation that a breakthrough might be made in U.S.-Iran relations. Iran also began trying to improve its relations with the Persian Gulf Arab states.

Two factors, however, prevented the success of this policy and later halted it. The first factor was the continued opposition and sabotage by the radicals. The second factor was the unresponsiveness of the West to Iranian overtures, which undermined the moderates. The Western position toward Iran in this period was that Iran had nowhere else to go and that if the West stood firm, Iran would accept all its conditions and normalize ties on Western terms.[88]

In addition, the West—especially the United States—argued that the changes in the Soviet Union and in East-West relations had reduced Iran's strategic and political significance. Indeed, the West believed that in view of Iraq's—and other Arabs'—larger oil reserves, they were much more important to the United States than Iran.

Thus, the West was not willing to offer Iran any incentives, whether in regard to the application of Resolution 598, the settlement of Iranian claims, or assistance for postwar reconstruction, which would have increased the chances of an Iran-West reconciliation. By January of 1989 the moderates' position had begun to erode, and Iran's policy of improving ties with the West had been stalled. There was a shift toward expanding ties with the Soviet Union and the Eastern bloc countries.

It was at this juncture that the Rushdie affair exploded. Salman Rushdie, an Indian-born British citizen, wrote a novel entitled *Satanic Verses*, satirizing the prophet of Islam, his wives, and other Islamic sanctities. The book, which appeared in the summer of 1988, was universally condemned by Muslims and led to protests and riots in many Muslim countries and communities, including the Indian subcontinent and England. The book was also condemned and banned by most Muslim governments, including Egypt and Saudi Arabia. Muslim leaders called for the execution of Rushdie.

For most of the summer and fall of 1988, Iran's reaction to the Rushdie affair was muted because the country was reeling under the trauma of the U.S. military strike and the cease-fire with Iraq. But by winter the Rushdie affair had become entangled with Iran's domestic politics and the intraregime struggle for power. The radicals, who were unhappy about the moderates' ascendancy and their open door policy to the West, used the Rushdie affair to undermine their position and policy. And the West's overreaction, as had often been the case in the past, played into the radicals' hands.

The radicals brought Rushdie's book to the attention of the Ayatollah Khomeini who, finding Rushdie guilty of apostasy, issued an edict calling for his death, a punishment prescribed by the Qur'an. Some lesser religious figures also offered a reward of $1 million for whoever killed Rushdie.

The Western governments, especially the United Kingdom, where Rushdie was a citizen, were understandably incensed by this edict. Some of Iran's moderate leaders, to prevent a serious deterioration of Iran's relations with the European countries, tried to make a distinction between the position of the Iranian government and the Ayatollah Khomeini's edict, characterizing it as a purely religious matter. These efforts failed. The Western countries, conscious of Iran's diminished strategic value in the post–Cold War era and its vast economic and financial needs, decided on a hard-line policy. Even the Federal Republic of Germany, which among the Western countries had maintained the closest ties with Iran, adopted a tough line. The European Community (EC) members recalled their ambassadors from Iran and instituted restrictions on economic and financial transactions with Iran.

The worsening of Iran's relations with the West and the relative recovery of the radicals' position were followed by a dramatic improvement in Soviet-Iranian ties. This shift was first indicated by the visit of an Iranian delegation to Moscow in January of 1989, headed by the Ayatollah Javadi Amoli, who delivered the Ayatollah Khomeini's now-famous letter to Mikhail Gorbachev.[89] This visit was followed by the visit of the Soviet foreign minister, Eduard Shevardnadze, to Tehran in February 1989, during which he was received by the Ayatollah Khomeini — a very rare occurrence. This visit and Hodjat-al-Islam Rafsanjani's later visit to Moscow when he met with Gorbachev would inaugurate a new stage in the long history of Russo-Iranian ties. During Rafsanjani's trip, wide-ranging agreements on economic cooperation were reached. The Soviets even agreed to meet some of Iran's defense needs, indeed delivering to Iran a squadron of MiG 29s in 1990.

Yet, as discussed below, the Soviet Union's effective disintegration and economic and other problems do not make Iran's strategy of closer economic ties with the USSR and other East European countries a very attractive option. At any rate, this strategy cannot eliminate Iran's need for Western capital and technology as the radicals might have hoped.

The Rushdie affair and the temporary ascendancy of the radicals also wasted any opportunity in early 1989 for a significant improvement in U.S.-Iran relations.

Although the United States in 1989 was no more willing than in 1988 to make any significant concessions to Iran, whether on the application of Resolution 598 or the settlement of Iranian claims, nevertheless, the tone of the new Bush administration toward Iran was more conciliatory. In fact, President George Bush, referring in his inaugural speech to the continued captivity of U.S. citizens by Lebanese groups with ties to Iran, indicated that if the hostages were released unconditionally, the U.S. attitude toward Iran would change. He sent this message to the Iranian leaders by saying that "good will begets good will."

Even without the radical backlash, the prospects for vastly improved U.S.-Iran relations would have remained, at best, mixed. The underlying premises of the Bush administration's approach to Iran were similar to those of the Reagan administration, namely: Iran is not important compared with Iraq and the Gulf Arabs; "no war, no peace" on the Iran-Iraq front is the best condition; Iran has nowhere else to go and will come to the United States on U.S. terms.

In short, during this period, Iran's domestic politics, coupled with dramatic changes at the international level, prevented the development and application of a coherent and consistent foreign policy. Its domestic policies also made the outside world less responsive to Iran's periodic signs of willingness to pursue a pragmatic, open, and even-handed foreign policy and to mend its relations with the West.

The Ayatollah Khomeini's Death and the Rafsanjani Presidency

During the first few weeks following the death of the founder of the Islamic republic, Iran was preoccupied with mourning ceremonies and effecting a smooth transition of power. Thus, activity on the foreign policy front, with one notable exception, was muted. The exception was the visit to Moscow of Hashemi Rafsanjani, then-speaker of the Iranian parliament, and his meeting with Mikhail Gorbachev on June 20, 1989.

This trip to the Soviet Union, however, had more than foreign policy ramifications. In the context of Iranian politics, Hodjat-al-Islam Rafsanjani had been one of the most prominent proponents of a more balanced and pragmatic foreign policy for Iran. He, at times, had also been one of the most vocal critics of aspects of Soviet policy toward Iran, including its massive arming of Iraq with sophisticated weaponry.[90]

Meanwhile, despite fluctuations in the Soviet assessment of the Iranian scene and subsequent policy toward Iran, two goals of the Soviet Union had remained constant until the acceleration of the USSR's disintegration after the events of August 1991: (1) Iran's relations with the West, especially the United States, should not improve at the expense of ties with Moscow, and (2) Iran should be a special sphere of Soviet influence, at least economically.

Thus, Rafsanjani's trip to Moscow shortly before Iran's presidential elections, which he was favored to win, was to cement special ties that had been evolving between Iran and the Soviet Union and to assure the Soviets that these ties would remain secure during a Rafsanjani presidency.

Potential areas of tension in Soviet-Iranian relations remained, however. The principal source of conflict related to developments in the Soviet Union's Asian republics. In January–February 1990, a particularly tense situation that developed during the fighting between Soviet Azerbaijanis and Armenians brought Soviet troops into Baku, the capital of Soviet Azerbaijan. Iran was torn between the necessity of not antagonizing the Soviets and the desire to help Azerbaijani Muslims.

To preempt any Iranian efforts on behalf of the Soviet Azerbaijanis, Gorbachev warned Iran against any meddling in the crisis, following which Iran's foreign minister declared that Iran would not interfere in other countries' internal affairs.[91]

It was generally expected that Hodjat-al-Islam Rafsanjani, once elected to the presidency and once having reassured the Soviets about their relations with Iran, would set out to improve ties to the West. Iran's domestic scene, the West's continued unresponsiveness, and developments in the Middle East prevented a rapid and sustained movement toward better ties with the West.

Domestically, although Hodjat-al-Islam Rafsanjani was elected president, he was not in a position to return Iran to one-man rule. Rather, he faced a delicate task of forging a consensus on the most important issues facing the nation. Because many influential figures — including the new spiritual leader, the Ayatollah Khamenei — did not share his opinions on some issues, his freedom of action regarding foreign policy was limited. The Western, especially the U.S., attitude toward Rafsanjani's administration was that the West would not do anything to help him until he consolidated his power and proved his good will by such acts as obtaining the release of Western hostages.

Regional developments clouded the beginning of Rafsanjani's presidency even before he was sworn in. On July 28, 1989, Israeli forces abducted a Lebanese Shi'a leader by the name of Shaykh Abd-al-Karim Obeid, who reportedly was the leader of the pro-Iranian extremist Lebanese Muslims. In retaliation, the Lebanese extremists threatened to kill U.S. hostage Joseph Ciccipio if the Israelis did not release Shaykh Obeid.

This situation put Iran's newly elected president in an extremely difficult position. On the one hand, the United States warned Iran that it would hold the country responsible if any U.S. hostage were harmed. It also hinted at military retaliation against Iran by moving U.S. naval forces to its vicinity. After the trauma of both the 1988 U.S.-Iran confrontation and a delicate process of transition of power, the new president could not afford a military confrontation with the United States.

Iran had to respond cautiously, which it did. During a Friday prayer sermon on August 4, 1989, President Rafsanjani said the problem of Lebanon and the hostages had peaceful solutions.[92] Iran also used its influence in Lebanon to prevent the killing of Joseph Ciccipio. This time, unlike previous occasions, the United States was willing to acknowledge Iran's help. On the other hand, even the appearance of a too-conciliatory attitude toward the United States could have become a political liability for the new president. Moreover, radical personalities such as Hodjat-al-Islam Ali-Akbar Mohtashami were manipulating the crisis and using their ties to the Lebanese extremists to undermine the position of the new president.

The crisis was resolved; the life of Joseph Ciccipio was spared and the military confrontation between Iran and the United States was averted, even though Shaykh Obeid was not released. During the next few months, Iran tried to resolve the hostage situation. For several reasons, it failed, although one U.S. hostage, Robert Polhill, was released on April 22, 1990, and another, Frank Reed, on April 30, 1990.

The first reason Iran failed is that Iran's influence over the hostage takers, although substantial, was not complete. Some of the hostage takers have their own concerns, such as gaining the freedom of their relatives. Second, Syria, with considerably more influence in Lebanon than Iran, has had its own agenda and often prevented a resolution of the problem until it had obtained some credit for it or had achieved a particular purpose.[93] An example of this Syrian strategy occurred when Syria made it clear in September 1990 that the restoration of diplomatic ties between Iran and the United Kingdom would not guarantee the release of Terry Waite and other British hostages and that the British had first to resolve their differences with Syria.

Third, the United States was not willing to offer any incentives to Iran, even though the Iranians, realizing the U.S. government's domestic problems regarding any dealings on the hostage issues, emphasized the humanitarian aspect of the issue and demanded only that the United States use its influence to get certain prisoners released from Israel and Kuwait. In other words, the Western frame of mind continued to be: Iran is no longer important, it has nowhere else to go, and in due course, it will meet Western demands.

By early 1990, Iran's relations with the European countries, with the exception of Britain, began to improve, and EC ambassadors returned to Tehran. Britain, however, insisted that before bilateral relations could improve, the Iranian government would have to rescind the Ayatollah Khomeini's edict on Salman Rushdie as well as resolve a few other issues. Britain knew full well that no Iranian political or religious leader could rescind an edict of the Ayatollah Khomeini. Britain also hindered improvements in Iran-EC relations as much as it could.

Individual European countries, notably France and Italy, however, proceeded to expand their economic and diplo-

matic ties with Iran. Iran also continued a policy of improving its ties with the Persian Gulf Arab states, with the
exception of Saudi Arabia.[94]

On one principal area of interest – namely, the application of Resolution 598 and the signing of a peace treaty
with Iraq, Iran's diplomacy failed, despite mediation efforts
by some Persian Gulf Arab countries, including Oman. Iraq
remained adamant on its demand for full sovereignty over
the Shat-al-Arab (Arvand Rud). An Arab League summit
on May 30, 1990, ratified this position, which triggered a
bitter reaction from Tehran.[95]

On June 21, 1990, Iran was hit by one of the worst
earthquakes in its history. Given the dimensions of this
national catastrophe, it was clear that Iran by itself could
not cope with the problem. The issue of accepting aid and
from whom, however, soon became entangled with the
broader issues of foreign policy. The moderates tried to use
this opportunity to rally popular support for a more open
and balanced Iranian diplomacy. They saw this as a chance
to demonstrate to the people the tangible benefits of having
good relations with other countries.[96]

The danger in this strategy was that in the case of a
tepid response from the international community, the public's disappointment would have strengthened the radicals'
arguments and position. Nevertheless, the moderates took
the risk. Iran declared that it would accept aid from any
source, including the United States.

The international – especially Western – response, although not matching its efforts in similar disasters elsewhere, was generous. Among the Western nations, West
Germany and France provided most of the assistance. Even
such archrivals as Saudi Arabia sent generous help. The
moderates, indeed, used this response to emphasize the necessity of Iran improving its international ties.

In addition, the economic burden of rebuilding the
quake-hit areas increased Iran's need for external financial
and technical assistance, thus putting a great premium on
improved relations with the West and the international fi-

nancial institutions. Indeed, as far as the latter is concerned, for some time Iran had been courting the World Bank and the IMF. An IMF team had visited Iran in March 1990, and a World Bank team had come in the summer of 1990. Iran had declared its intention to seek the World Bank's technical expertise. Nevertheless, even with the trauma of the quake and the openings it created, the pace of improvement in Iran's relations with Western and Arab countries and the international organizations did not accelerate noticeably. This had to wait until the dramatic events of August 1990.

Iraq's Invasion of Kuwait: New Opportunities and Challenges for Iranian Foreign Policy

On August 2, 1990, after several weeks of tension and build-up of Iraqi military forces on the borders, Iraq invaded and occupied Kuwait, which led to the Persian Gulf crisis and the introduction of nearly half a million U.S. and other troops to the area. In an extremely rare instance of international cooperation, the world community sought to isolate Iraq economically and politically by imposing comprehensive trade sanctions and diplomatic pressures.

The Persian Gulf crisis had certain dividends for Iran. The most important was the Iraqi government's acceptance of Iran's peace terms, which included the recognition of joint sovereignty over the Shat-al-Arab as embodied in the Algiers agreement of 1975.

Getting its peace terms accepted was of great importance to the Islamic government, which politically could not have afforded unfavorable comparisons with the Pahlavi regime. Without peace, Iran's chances of economic revitalization would have been undermined. Thus, the obtaining of a respectable peace had been the primary goal of Iran's diplomacy, but none of the efforts, either through the UN's intermediary or through mediation by Persian Gulf Arab states such as Oman, had been very successful. An important breakthrough in this regard was the letter sent by the Iraqi president, Saddam Hussein, to Iran's president in May 1990, in which he stated that the continued hostility between Iran and Iraq benefited only the "arrogant powers"—meaning essentially the United States. He fell short, however, of admitting the applicability of the provisions of the Algiers agreement.

Iran responded positively but cautiously to these Iraqi overtures. It insisted that any peace negotiations and eventual peace treaty should be developed in the context of UN Security Council Resolution 598. Several preliminary meetings were held between Iranian and Iraqi experts and officials during June and July with the goal of preparing the ground for a summit meeting between Presidents Saddam Hussein and Rafsanjani. Nevertheless, during these contacts, Iraq was not willing to make concessions Tehran considered satisfactory. After invading Kuwait, and faced with the buildup of international forces in Saudi Arabia, however, Iraq needed to pacify its border with Iran and free its troops. Thus, on August 15 it accepted all of Iran's principal points.

This was an opportunity that the Iranian government could not let pass. On August 17, 1990, Iraqi troops began to pull out from Iranian territory. On the same day, the two countries began the exchange of prisoners. On September 10, 1990, the countries declared they would resume diplomatic relations, and on October 14, 1990, their embassies reopened. Iraq's invasion of Kuwait, while helping Iran to obtain peace on its terms, posed a number of dilemmas for Iran. To begin with, Iran could not look at Iraq's acquisition of Kuwait and the ensuing improvement in its wealth and geostrategic position without deep anxiety. In fact, Iran could not be sure that in case of victory over Kuwait, Iraq would not be again tempted to turn its attention to the Iranian province of Khusistan.

But even if Iraq were not to threaten Iran's territorial integrity, its emergence as the predominant power in the Persian Gulf and the Middle East could hardly be welcomed by Iran. Moreover, suddenly having discovered religion, Saddam Hussein was increasingly resorting to Islamic symbols and terminology in his speeches, making him a potential rival for the leadership of the Islamic world.

In addition, Saddam Hussein was increasingly linking the Palestinian problem and his invasion of Kuwait, and he was trying to barter Kuwait in exchange for Israel's withdrawal from occupied Arab territories. If he had succeeded in this goal – something to which Iran had also committed itself, at least rhetorically – he would have become an unquestioned hero and thus an unbeatable rival.

Consequently, Iran could not acquiesce in Iraq's takeover of Kuwait or help it in any significant way to circumvent the international embargo. Equally important, any acquiescence in this regard would have scuttled all of Iran's diplomatic strategy of improving its ties with the West and obtaining financial and technical assistance.

In addition, some of Iran's Arab allies (such as Syria, which had sided with Iran during its war with Iraq) had joined the Western powers in opposing Iraq. Any sign of Iranian willingness to help Iraq would have deeply antagonized Syria.

Even more seriously, if it had been willing to cooperate with Iraq, Iran itself could have faced economic embargo; the United States hinted that it would seek UN sanctions against countries that broke the embargo against Iraq. But to go too far against Iraq would have jeopardized Iran's chances of obtaining a favorable peace, in addition to other liabilities, both domestically and in the region.

Domestically, certain hard-liners, including Hodjat-al-Islam Mohtashami and Ayatollah Sadegh Khalkhali, had been arguing for cooperation with Iraq against the United States. Iran's eagerness to sign a peace treaty with Iraq and to secure the withdrawal of Iraqi forces from its territory was interpreted in the West as another sign of Iranian villainy. The West had hoped that Iran, by refusing to sign a peace treaty, would keep a large number of Iraqi forces occupied so that they would not be sent to Kuwait.

What was forgotten, however, was that it was the Western preference for a state of "no war, no peace" on the Iran-Iraq front and its unwillingness to help implement UN Security Council Resolution 598 that had left Iran with no choice but to seize the Iraqi peace offer. Given the strategy used by Saddam Hussein to wrap himself and his actions in the flag of Palestinian and Islamic rights, Iran could not adopt a too pro-West and too strident anti-Iraq policy. Furthermore, the anti-Saddam movement was led by the United States, and Iran politically could not afford to be identified too closely with U.S. efforts.

Thus, Iran adopted a two-pronged and fairly balanced policy on the Kuwait problem. It condemned categorically Iraq's invasion of Kuwait and voted for the UN resolution calling for Iraqi withdrawal and the restoration of Kuwait's legitimate government. It complied with the sanctions reasonably faithfully. It pursued peace and the normalization of relations with Iraq.

There was one more reason for this Iranian attitude. Iran could not be certain that the United States and its allies could eliminate Saddam Hussein, and Iran suspected that the allies might be willing to accept a compromise solution that would have left Iran to face an even more vengeful Iraq. Indeed, despite a devastating and punishing war, Saddam was still in power at the end of 1991.Domestic politics also argued in favor of a cautious policy and against a policy of wholeheartedly joining the U.S.-led coalition. Even Iran's spiritual leader, the Ayatollah Khamenei, called for a holy war against U.S. troops in Saudi Arabia. These radical outpourings were quickly silenced; it was evident, however, that Iran's domestic politics would not allow a bolder policy.

Problematic as the situation created by the Iraqi invasion of Kuwait and the introduction of foreign, especially U.S., forces to the area was from the Iranian perspective, Iran faced even more severe dilemmas after the crisis.

As noted, Iran could not be comfortable with an Iraqi victory that made Iraq the dominant power. At the same time, total destruction of Iraq and the establishment of what Iran saw as U.S.-Saudi hegemony and the permanent establishment of U.S. ground forces in Saudi Arabia and other Persian Gulf Arab states were viewed as threatening by Tehran. Rightly or wrongly, the Iranian regime believes that the United States has not yet come to terms with it and, if possible, would encourage a change of regime.

In addition, Iran believed that a U.S.-Saudi hegemony would isolate Iran and exclude it from playing a meaningful role in the Gulf region and beyond. This is the reason Iran responded negatively to the statement by U.S. Secretary of State James Baker about the possibility of creating a security framework for the Persian Gulf modeled on the North Atlantic Treaty Organization. Thus, Iran, while demanding the withdrawal of Iraqi troops from all of Kuwait, also called for a peaceful solution to the Persian Gulf crisis. Iran also tried its own regional diplomacy – with some success.

One of the most significant gains for Iran from Iraq's aggression was a kind of moral victory vis-à-vis the Persian Gulf Arabs who had applauded Iraq's aggression against Iran and bankrolled its war effort. In fact, after the invasion, Kuwait's foreign minister, who was visiting Iran, expressed regret at Kuwait's past support for Iraq.[97]

Iran's relations with Oman have always been good, except for a few brief years after the revolution. Oman has always looked at Iran as a counterweight to Saudi Arabia, toward which Oman has some misgivings. Relations between the two countries have been improving since the end of the Iran-Iraq War. As noted, Oman was active in mediating between Iran and Iraq. Before the Iraqi invasion of Kuwait, there was talk of a summit meeting between Presidents Hashemi Rafsanjani and Saddam Hussein in Oman. An Iranian naval vessel made a courtesy visit to Oman, and the two countries have reached a number of agreements to cooperate economically and culturally.

Relations between Iran and the United Arab Emirates (UAE) have also been good. Since the Iraqi invasion, relations between Iran and Bahrain have been improving. There were even contacts between Iranian and Saudi officials. Iran has also been improving ties with the newly unified Yemen.[98]

More broadly, Iran began discussing with the Persian Gulf Arab states the issue of regional security in the Persian Gulf once the crisis was over. Iran opposes the presence of other, especially U.S., forces in the Persian Gulf. Iran's position in this regard is that regional security should be the responsibility of the littoral states. But according to some reports, Iran at one point suggested that Turkey and Pakistan may be part of a Persian Gulf security system.[99]

Iran's regional diplomacy scored a success when Gulf Cooperation Council (GCC) members declared after their summit meeting that the GCC welcomed better ties with Iran and that Iran should be included in any future regional security system.[100]

Immediately after the end of hostilities between Iraq and the U.S.-led coalition forces, however, it appeared that key members of the coalition would prefer to keep Iran out of future security arrangements. After a meeting with Syria's minister of foreign affairs, for example, British Foreign Secretary Douglas Hurd said that postwar Gulf security should be "mainly Arab-led."[101]

Later, on March 5, 1991, when the representatives of six Persian Gulf Arab countries met with Syrian and Egyptian representatives in Damascus and issued the Damascus Declaration, it appeared that a future Persian Gulf security framework would be built around the GCC, plus Egypt and Syria, or the so-called six plus two formula.[102]

After the Damascus meeting, the secretary-general of the GCC made a vague statement to the effect that the Persian Gulf Arab states must reach some kind of understanding with Iran. It is important to note here that not all Gulf Arabs wanted to keep Iran out of the security arrangements. In fact, Oman and the UAE strongly supported Iran's inclusion in the security arrangements. Some Western countries, such as France, were also of this view.

Understandably, Iran, particularly its press, reacted

negatively to these events. But the Iranian government's policy remained low-key and nonconfrontational, and Iran pursued its policy of reconciliation with the Arab world.

As a result, Iran reestablished full diplomatic relations with Tunisia and Jordan. Relations with Egypt improved, and the two countries opened interest sections in each other's capitals. Most important was the resumption of diplomatic relations with Saudi Arabia on March 19, 1991, and the compromise reached between the two countries on the issue of the Iranian pilgrims to Mecca.

For the remainder of 1991, regional politics related to the Persian Gulf and the Arab-Israeli conflict experienced rapid, often contradictory, shifts. During the spring and summer of 1991, for example, the early euphoria about the creation of a new regional security order based on the twin pillars of close inter-Arab and U.S.-Arab cooperation began to dissipate as age-old Arab rivalries and certain fundamental barriers to a tight U.S.-Arab identification reasserted themselves. Egypt, disappointed at the low level of Gulf Arab aid and also reportedly angry at the Gulf Arabs' unwillingness to exclude Iran completely from regional affairs, declared on March 8, 1991, that it would withdraw its 38,000 troops from Kuwait. The Gulf Arabs, for their part, seemed to be having second thoughts about the wisdom of having such large numbers of Arab troops on their soil.

Syria's expectations of a dramatic shift in U.S. policy toward the Arab-Israeli conflict were also disappointed, and it tried to reaffirm its ties with Iran. On April 28, 1991, during President Rafsanjani's visit to Syria, the Syrians departed from the terms of the Damascus Declaration and declared that Iran should be involved in the Gulf security plans.[103]

Saddam Hussein's continuing power in Iraq, despite the decimation of his military, the devastation of his country, and widespread revolt and civil war, also affected Arab calculations and enhanced Iran's value as the regional counterweight to Iraq. Iran could thus take some comfort in the reassertion of its geostrategic and political importance in the region despite earlier expectations. Still, the future of Persian Gulf security and Iran's role in it remained uncertain.

Indeed, the evolution of regional politics presented a mixed picture for Iran's aspirations that posed delicate dilemmas. In the Persian Gulf, despite some early difficulties, the United States had signed security agreements with Kuwait and Bahrain and was also envisaging similar arrangements with the United Arab Emirates. The Gulf states' actions, which were clearly in defiance of Iran, put the Iranian government in a delicate position, especially given that hard-liners in the parliament and the press had begun attacking the Gulf Arab leaders. If the government had overreacted to these developments, its entire strategy of developing cooperative relations with the Persian Gulf Arab states would have been jeopardized; yet domestic politics required some expression of displeasure. The government's attitude reflected the growing realism of Iranian diplomacy: The Kuwaiti ambassador to Iran was summoned to the Foreign Ministry, but no other action detrimental to Iran's relations with the Gulf states was taken.

The trend toward improving Iran's Gulf ties continued. In September, Iran's foreign minister met with the emir of Kuwait, who was also attending the UN General Assembly meeting in New York City. In the same month, the foreign ministers of the Gulf Cooperation Council and the Iranian foreign minister met to discuss issues related to Persian Gulf security and Iran's role, as well as cooperation between Iran and the GCC. Following these contacts, the foreign minister of Saudi Arabia Prince Saud Bin Faisal told reporters that if current positive trends in Iran's diplomacy continued, Iran and the GCC could develop mutually beneficial relations during the 1990s. Later, it was reported that King Fahd had extended an invitation to President Rafsanjani to visit Saudi Arabia. Another sign of improved relations with the Gulf countries was the visit of the crown prince of Qatar to Tehran in November. These movements indicated that Iran's leadership had accepted the realities of the post–cold war and post–Gulf war period, including the U.S. strategic supremacy in the region, even if it was unable or unwilling to admit it openly. They also indicated that Iran had decided to promote its interests through a realistic diplomacy under the new international conditions.

Another development that posed dilemmas for Iran was the U.S. success in finally bringing the Arabs, including the Palestinians, and Israel together around the peace table in Madrid on October 30, 1991. Moreover, the peace process was not limited this time to the Arab-Israeli conflict, but envisaged parallel multilateral negotiations on such broader issues as arms control, resource management, development, and environmental protection. Iran's domestic politics, however, prevented it from taking part in this process. Indeed, there was an outpouring of radical and highly inflammatory rhetoric from Iranian hard-liners, and Tehran hosted a conference on October 19 in which radical rejectionist forces from the region and other Muslim countries took part. This Iranian attitude contrary to the general conciliatory, pragmatic trend of Iran's diplomacy and damaging to its interests was prompted largely by domestic politics, especially pressure from the hard-liners; it was also a reaction to what appeared to be Iran's isolation and marginalization in the region – that is, an effort to show that Iran was a country to be reckoned with and that its pragmatism and moderation should not be taken for granted.

Although Iran continued to adhere to uncompromising rhetoric on the Arab-Israeli conflict, later developments showed that the Tehran conference did not indicate a major departure from the pragmatic policy of the Rafsanjani administration. Rather, it was more an aberration prompted mainly by domestic politics. The most notable development was Iran's determination to end the hostage issue. In fact,

Iran had been working for some time with the UN secretary general to end the hostage crisis. This time around, different international and regional conditions, especially the coinciding of Syrian and Iranian interest in ending the crisis, led to more success. Indeed, Iranian officials expressed confidence that the hostage file would be closed by the end of 1991.

Iran's relations with Europe also benefited from the Persian Gulf crisis. Iraq's invasion of Kuwait illustrated the fallacy of the theory that Iran lacked strategic importance in the post–cold war era, as well as the folly of weakening Iran beyond what was necessary and building up Iraq.

Iran's position as the largest country with the largest coastline in the Persian Gulf makes it the natural and most viable counterweight to Iraq. In the spring of 1991, with Iran's "open door" policy toward Kurdish refugees fleeing Saddam's repression and its generous assistance to them, Iran's image in Europe improved further. Thus, the European countries moved to consolidate relations with Iran. In November 1990, the European Community canceled all remaining sanctions on Iran and declared its decision to open a permanent representation in Tehran. Even Britain, which had insisted on the freedom of British hostages and the rescinding of the Ayatollah Khomeini's death edict on Salman Rushdie before restoring ties with Iran, believed it necessary to be more flexible.

The Rushdie problem with Britain, as well as with other EC countries, was resolved through an exchange of letters. The European countries agreed to be respectful of Islam, and Iran reiterated its commitment to observe international rules and regulations. As a result, Britain and Iran resumed diplomatic relations on September 27, 1990. Britain's freeing of an Iranian student, Mehrdad Kowkabi, in mid-March 1991 and the release of British businessman Roger Cooper by Iran in early April improved the context of British-Iranian relations. British authorities made it clear, however, that a dramatic improvement in relations could not be expected until the release of the British hostages held in Lebanon. But the release of two British hostages in August and November 1991 should remove all barriers to better ties.

The tempo of Franco-Iranian reconciliation quickened and culminated in the visit of Iran's foreign minister to France in early December, when he also met with the French president, François Mitterrand.[104] French Foreign Minister Roland Dumas then visited Tehran on May 3, 1991, and a meeting between President Rafsanjani and President Mitterrand was anticipated in the near future. The French government postponed the visit indefinitely, however, when former Iranian Prime Minister Shahpour Bakhtiar was assassinated in Paris by individuals allegedly linked to the Iranian government.[105] The German foreign minister also visited Iran on May 6, 1991, and extended an invitation to President Rafsanjani to visit Bonn.[106] Relations with the United States, although eased a bit, remained tense.

The most important point about the evolution of Iran's foreign policy in the post-Khomeini era is that the pragmatic and realist trend has been strengthened. Also, Iran's foreign policy has acquired an increasingly statist and nationalist character in the sense that Iran's national interest, rather than vague ideological principles, has become the guiding force.

Disagreements on foreign policy orientation still exist and often complicate the task of Iranian diplomacy. The regime's ideology, although much diluted, is still constraining its diplomacy and its ability to maximize the country's national interest. By refusing to negotiate with the United States, for example, the regime is denying Iran a more important regional position, thus allowing peripheral countries to supplant it in the region. As long as the domestic political debate is not resolved and a solid majority view formed, these problems will bedevil Iran's foreign policy.

The problem of U.S. hostages in Lebanon also continued to be a serious barrier to better U.S.-Iran ties. But with the release of three U.S. hostages in August and November and the release of the remaining hostages by the end of 1991, prospects for some improvement in U.S.-Iran ties seemed more encouraging.

Other factors besides domestic politics have constrained Iran's diplomacy, especially its ability to achieve a breakthrough in relations with the United States. One major constraint has been U.S. unwillingness to do its part to improve ties with Iran. With an eye to postcrisis politics, the United States found it expedient during the Persian Gulf crisis to continue to portray Iran as a major threat to regional security. In theory this could be useful in justifying the permanent stationing of U.S. military forces in the region.

The United States may find this strategy useful in justifying a policy of rewarding Turkey and Egypt by according them a significant role in the Persian Gulf. Also, the United States may still think that exaggerating the Iranian threat and encouraging Arab-Iranian tensions could induce the Arabs to reach a compromise with Israel. Although this approach failed when it was the cornerstone of U.S. policy toward Iran in the period after the Iran-contra episode, the forces that led to the adoption of this policy still had influence in the region and within the U.S. bureaucracy.

As the inadvisability of this policy becomes evident to the United States, however, and as Iran sees the foolishness of ignoring a great power such as the United States and, more important, continues to moderate its domestic politics, the chances of a significant amelioration in U.S.-Iran ties will increase. In fact, despite public animosity, regular communications between the United States and Iran increased during and after the Persian Gulf War. The U.S. government has not completely closed the door to Iranian participation in Persian Gulf security provided, of course, U.S.-Iran relations improve. In particular, President Bush on several occasions has noted that Iran should not be forever considered as a pariah.

There also was some easing of trade restrictions on

both sides. Indeed, U.S.-Iran bilateral trade increased considerably in 1991. Although full normalization of U.S.-Iran relations would take a long time, Iran's pragmatic diplomacy and the release of U.S. hostages in Lebanon give cause for optimism about somewhat better relations in the not-too-distant future.

Conclusions and Outlook

What conclusions about the enduring features of Iran's national and cultural life, as well as its future evolution, can be drawn from the foregoing analysis? Perhaps the most significant is the degree of Iran's resilience and the strength of its survival instinct as a country and nation. The experience of the past decade, for example, has proven wrong those observers who viewed Iran as a fractious multinational entity without a strong and broad-based sense of its cultural and political identity and a developed sense of national wholeness. No doubt, there are strong centrifugal tendencies in Iran, but elements of national unity are also very strong. The behavior of the overwhelming majority of the Iranians of all ethnic and linguistic groups during the Iran-Iraq War and their rallying in defense of their country was a critical test of this sense of collective commitment to Iran as the territorial and cultural expression of the Iranian people.

Particularly instructive in this regard was the behavior of Iran's so-called Arab population. After Iraq's occupation of Khusistan, this group left their devastated homeland and settled in other parts of Iran rather than joining the Iraqis or fleeing to Iraq. Nor, outside of the most extreme of ethnic separatist elements, was there any significant movement on the part of Iran's ethnic and linguistic minorities to take advantage of the central government's problems and launch separatist movements. This experience indicates that although Iran's problems of national cohesion are not eliminated, its chances of survival as a territorial and national unit in the future are quite strong, unless the whole region undergoes significant territorial readjustment as a result of outside intervention. Such readjustment is now a real possibility—in particular, the long-term consequences of the Kurdish problem in Iraq could affect the region's map. Even in that case, however, Iran's chances of maintaining its current borders are stronger than some of the region's other countries.

The experience of the last decade has also illustrated once more the importance and relevance of Iran's past for the country's current political and cultural life and vision of the outside world. Of particular importance in this regard has been the clear demonstration of how Iran's pre-Islamic past and Islam have been blended during several centuries to form a unique Iranian and Islamic cultural identity. It has also become clear how futile and short-lived are any efforts to separate these two important components of Iranian culture or give one precedence over the other.

The reemergence of Iranianism in Iran and the Islamic regime's recognition—albeit grudging—of the importance of this aspect of Iranian culture and identity prove this assertion. This trend, barring significant developments outside Iran and, in particular, another outbreak of Islamic revivalism, is likely to continue and deepen. This, however, does not mean a dramatic reversal and the replacement of the present view by a purely secular nationalist one that does not represent Iranian national identity either. Rather, it means the restoration of the balance between Islam and Iranianism and a new synthesis of the two, which would be more representative of the true character of Iran's national identity and more in tune with the majority's preferences.

This phenomenon would affect how Iran defines its place in the outside world, as well as its view of where its interests lie. In particular, it would strengthen a nationalist approach to conducting Iran's foreign policy in the sense that Iran's national interests would have priority over vague ideological goals, a trend that has been evident for some time. Indeed, recent trends in Iran could be characterized as "statism" and "Iran Firstism." This does not mean Iran will lose interest in the fate of Islam or Muslim causes but that it would pursue these goals in ways that would not harm its national interests.

Other aspects of Iran's past and political culture, including Iran's view of itself as a major regional force, have historically colored its world view and thus the conduct of its foreign relations. These influences, evident even behind Islamic symbolism, would further reassert themselves. Iran's attitude toward the future regional security system for the Persian Gulf and Iran's place in it reveals the influence of past experiences on Iran's behavior.

Events of the past decade, particularly following Ayatollah Khomeini's death, have shown the resilience and tenacity of the Islamic regime, despite inherent and fundamental weaknesses. They also reveal, as does the smooth transference of power, the adaptability and flexibility of the political institutions and processes of the Islamic government.

Iran's process of transferring power, its constitutional reform, and its increasingly more collegial and consensual politics and decision making show that Iran's political system is in many ways more mature than those of many other Middle Eastern countries where the elimination of one individual of much less significance than Iran's Khomeini could derail politics and governance for a long time or result in military rule.

The same experience and events also point to fundamental weaknesses of the regime deriving from the contradictions and ambiguities inherent in its theological and legal foundations and the deep philosophical divisions within its leadership. They also highlight two principal dilemmas of the regime.

First, to survive and prosper, the regime must reform and adapt itself to the imperatives of running an effective government that is indispensable to Iran's economic revitalization and international rehabilitation. But, in the process, the regime must accept a dilution of its more revolutionary characteristics and the gradual broadening of the base of the current political and professional elite in power and the possible loss of certain constituencies.

Second, to succeed, the reformist elements of the regime must isolate the extremist elements and find new political partners so they can dispense with the radicals. But they face a very difficult task. Opposition groups are unlikely to cooperate with them without significant concessions in terms of political reforms and easing of social and cultural rigors that could be unacceptable to even the most moderate and reform-minded members of the regime.

The regime may be helped, however, by two factors, should it choose to follow in this path. First, barring external developments, no single opposition or even a coalition of various opposition groups is currently in a position to challenge the regime seriously. Second, if the moderate elements of the regime improve the economy and stabilize the political scene, many opposition groups may be tempted to cooperate with the government.

If the regime cannot reform itself and broaden its base of support, its internal divisions would gravely undermine its ability to revitalize Iran economically and politically. This would lead to growing popular dissatisfaction that, combined with intraregime divisions, could destabilize the country and threaten the regime's political survival. The outcome of such a scenario, however, is likely to be sustained political chaos rather than a clear victory for one opposition group or a return to the prerevolution political setup. Hence, developments in the next few years are vital for Iran's future. They will test the ability of Iranian moderates to pursue a policy of economic, political, social, and cultural reform in Iran. If they succeed, Iran will be the first country to provide a model of a progressive and democratic system of Islamic government and society at peace with itself and with the world. No assessment, however, of the moderates' chances of succeeding in this task can be accurate.

In addition to internal difficulties on the way to reform and the daunting dimensions of the economic challenge the regime faces, the regime's and Iran's fate will be largely determined by events beyond Iran's control. Particularly significant in this regard are the unfolding events in Soviet Asia and their regional repercussions. Of even more immediate impact are the long-term consequences of the Persian Gulf War.

In short, 12 years after the Iranian revolution and 3 years after the demise of the founder of the Islamic republic, Iran's future course is not clear. The Islamic regime is poised on a threshold, and its leadership faces a basic choice: It can reform and transform itself into a more open, progressive, tolerant Islamic state relevant to the challenges of Iran and the world in the twenty-first century. Failing that, it would risk alienating vast numbers of Iranians; such widespread alienation, combined with the deep divisions in Iranian society, could dangerously undermine the Islamic regime's survival. In the latter case, however, no single opposition or one particular political view is likely to emerge as the natural successor. Rather, Iran would in all likelihood plunge into another period of political turmoil marked by rivalries among various political forces. The outcome of such a scenario cannot be predicted at this point, either for the character of future regimes in Iran or even for its survival as a nation within its current boundaries.

The regime must be able to address Iran's economic problems effectively, particularly the dilemma of how to reconcile the requirements of economic efficiency with those of social justice and provide for a more participatory and responsive system of government. Furthermore, the current regime or any other prospective regime must adopt a realistic view of Iran's underlying historical and cultural forces and be able to discern and manage the dynamics of its strategic environment. In the coming months and years, the skill of Iranian diplomacy would be critical to ensuring Iran's survival and future success. At the time this monograph was completed, Iran's internal developments, the conduct of its foreign policy, and the leadership skills of President Rafsanjani, combined with his determination to pursue a reformist path in domestic and foreign policy, give cause, more than at any other time since Iran's revolution, for cautious optimism about Iran's future.

Notes

1. For a brief analysis of Iran's prerevolution constitution, see Richard F. Nyrop, ed., *Iran: A Country Study* (Washington, D.C.: The American University, 1978), 179–199.

2. The 1906 constitution was largely modeled after the Belgian constitution.

3. Those involved in urban guerrilla warfare and other subversive activities included the Islamo-Marxist Mujaheddin-e-Khalq and the secular Marxist Fedayan-e-Khalq. Many of them received training and financial support from radical Arab states and the Palestine Liberation Organization (PLO) and thus indirectly from the Soviet Union.

4. For an excellent analysis of the interaction between Iran's pre-Islamic past and Islam, see *En Islam Iranien*, 4 vols. (Paris: Gallimard, 1972). In particular, see the discussion on Shayk Shahab-ed-Din Sohrawardi and his philosophy of Ishragh, which is inspired by pre-Islamic Iranian Mazdaic traditions and philosophy.

5. Because of this interdependence, for example, some Arabs have portrayed Shi'ism as an Iranian conspiracy against Islam. See Hamid Enayat, "Iran and the Arabs," in Sylvia Haim, ed., *Arab Nationalism and a Wider World* (New York: American Association for Peace in the Middle East, 1971), 13–25.

6. Alexander's conquest (331 B.C.) was followed, for example, by a rebirth of Iranian dynasties such as the Arsacids (129 B.C.–226 A.D.) and the Sassanids (226 A.D.–642 A.D.) and a new Irani-

an cultural renaissance. The Arab invasion (c. 642 C.E.) was followed by a literary and cultural renaissance. Iran even withstood recurring Mongol and Turkic invasions and managed to regain its territorial integrity and assert its cultural identity under the Safavids.

7. For an analysis of this phenomenon, see two works by Fereydoun Adamiyat: *Andishehay-e-Mirza Agha Khan Kirmani* (The thoughts of Mirza Agha Khan Kirmani) (Tehran: Chapkhaneh Pirouz, 1346 [1967]), and *Fakr-e-Azadi Va Nehzat-e-Mashrutiat* (The idea of freedom and the constitutional movement) (Tehran: Entesharat-e-Sokhan, 1340 [1962]).

8. The first efforts at reform started during the Russo-Iranian wars (1804–1828) when Abbas Mirza Qajar, Iran's crown prince, sent the first group of Iranian students abroad. The most systematic but short-lived reforms were carried out by Mirza Taghi Khan Farahani (Amir Kabir), Iranian prime minister from 1846 to 1851. See Fereydoun Adamiyat, *Amir Kabir Va Iran* (Tehran: Chapkhaneh Payam, 1323 [1944–1945]).

9. In his aforementioned book *The Idea of Freedom and the Constitutional Movement*, Adamiyat mentions a work by an unknown author who attributes Iran's sorry state to disregard for Islamic principles. He complains that because of this neglect, the Iranians are forced to import Christian laws.

10. For an analysis of the impact of Western ideas on Iran's intellectual development during the nineteenth and twentieth centuries, in addition to the aforementioned works by Adamiyat, see the following work by the same author: *Andisheh-e-Taraghi Va Hokoumat-e-Ghanoun: Assr-e-Sepah Solar* (The idea of progress and the rule of law) (Tehran: Entesharat-e-Kharazim, 1351 [1973]).

11. Many prominent Shi'a religious men (*alim*), including Mohammad Bagher Majlesi and Shaykh Koleini, have produced Hadiths from Shi'a imams on why the Iranians are superior to the Arabs in matters of faith. Irrespective of the veracity of such Hadiths, this phenomenon shows an effort to reconcile the Iranian and Islamic dimensions of Iran's national identity. See Hamid Enayat, *Modern Islamic Political Thought* (Austin: University of Texas Press, 1982).

12. One enlightened *alim* who recognized the necessity of reform, including political reform, in Iran was the Ayatollah Mirza Hossein Naini, a supporter of constitutionalism.

13. On the Ayatollah Khomeini's views on this subject, see Farhang Rajaee, *Islamic Values and World View: Khomeini on Man, the State, and International Politics* (New York: University Press of America, 1983), 56–58. In 1943, for example, the Ayatollah wrote that "the ulama never wanted to destroy the foundation of the government. . . . They have never to this day opposed the principal foundation of monarchy. In fact, most of the great ulama . . . accompanied and assisted the monarch . . . [p. 57]."

14. For the text of the Ayatollah Khomeini's letters, see *Foreign Broadcasting Information Service (FBIS)*, April 25, 1989, pp. 61–62.

15. For a discussion of this issue and other issues related to constitutional reform, see the commentary in the daily *Resalat*, published in *FBIS/NES*, July 27, 1989, pp. 43–61.

16. Ibid., 48.

17. See "Elections Renew Factional Fighting," *Iran Focus* 3, no. 10 (November 1990): 2.

18. The radicals accused the Ayatollah Khamenei of reactionary thinking, and Hodjat-al-Islam Mohtashmi implied that the Ayatollah Khamenei and Rafsanjani were enemies of the revolution. "Factional Disputes Take to Streets," *Iran Focus* 3, no. 10 (November 1990): 2.

19. See the discussion in *Resalat*, *FBIS/NES*, July 27, 1989, p. 49.

20. For the text of the *Tehran Times* article, see *FBIS/NES*, May 25, 1989, pp. 37–38.

21. For an elaboration of these points, see Shireen T. Hunter, "After the Ayatollah," *Foreign Policy*, no. 66 (Spring 1987): 77–97, and "Post Khomeini Iran," *Foreign Affairs* 68, no. 5 (Winter 1989/90), 133–149.

22. For the relevant parts of Velayati's speech, see *Washington Post*, November 27, 1986, p. A27.

23. For Rafsanjani's cabinet, see *FBIS/NES*, August 21, 1989, pp. 51–52.

24. On the parliamentary debate on cabinet, see *FBIS/NES*, August 20, 1989, p. 41.

25. For the text of Rafsanjani's speech, see *FBIS/NES*, August 24, 1989, pp. 42–47.

26. For the principal points of the bill and parliamentary debate on it, see "Majlis Commission Debates Security Forces Merger," *FBIS/NES*, June 21, 1990, pp. 48–51.

27. On the military before the revolution and the transition from the monarchy to the Islamic regime, see Sepehr Zabih, *The Iranian Military in War and Revolution* (London & New York: Rutledge & Chapman & Hall, 1988).

28. On these issues, see William F. Hickman, *Ravaged and Reborn: The Iranian Army* (Washington, D.C.: The Brookings Institution, 1982).

29. On the purges, see Hickman, *Ravaged and Reborn*, and Nikola B. Schahgaldian, *The Iranian Military under the Islamic Republic* (Santa Monica, Calif.: RAND Corporation, 1987), 64–86.

30. See Shireen T. Hunter, "The Iran-Iraq War and Iran's Defense Policy," *Gulf Security and the Iran-Iraq War*, Thomas Naff, ed. (Washington, D.C.: National Defense University Press, 1985), 157–182.

31. For further information, see "U.S. Spy Ring Broken," *Middle East Economic Digest* (hereafter *MEED*) 33, no. 17 (May 5, 1989): 22.

32. For a comparison of Iran's military forces with those of its neighbors, see *The Military Balance 1990–1991* (London: International Institute for Strategic Studies, 1990).

33. On the delivery of Soviet aircraft, see "Moscow Signals Shift with MIG-29 Delivery," *MEED* 34, no. 39 (October 5, 1990): 14.

34. See the statement by Defense and Logistics Minister Akbar Torkan about using excess capacity in military factories to produce nondefense goods. *MEED* 33, no. 35 (September 8, 1989): 24.

35. On the income distribution gap, see Masoud Kavoosi, "The Post-Revolutionary Iranian Economy: Opportunities and Constraints," *Business Economics* 22, no. 2 (April 9, 1988): 35. Also, Hooshang Amirahmadi, *Revolution and Economic Transition: The Iranian Experience* (Albany, N.Y.: State University of New York Press, 1990), 194–199.

36. On the prerevolution planning in Iran, see Kamran Mofid, *Development Planning in Iran from Monarchy to Islamic Republic* (Outwell, Wisbech, Cambridgeshire, England: Middle East and North African Studies Press, 1987).

37. On Islam's view of economics, see Sohrab Behdad, "The Political Economy of Islamic Planning in Iran," in Hooshang Amirahmadi and Manoucher Parvin, eds., *Post-Revolutionary Iran* (Boulder, Colo.: Westview Press, 1988), 107–125.

38. See Rajaee, *Islamic Values and World View*, 22.

39. On the politics of economic planning related to land reform, see Shaul Bakhash, "The Politics of Land, Law, and Social Justice in Iran," *Middle East Journal* 43, no. 2 (Spring 1989): 186–201.

40. For more details, see the text of the plan.

41. For a brief but good analysis of the problems and potential of Iran's agriculture, see *Iran Yearbook 1989/90* (Bonn, West Germany: MOB Publishing Company, Ltd.), 15-5, 16-3.

42. These dams included Karaj, Lar, Safid Rud, Aras, and Karun.

43. For a more detailed analysis, see Amirahmadi, *Revolution and Economic Transition*, 197–199.

44. Ibid., 203–207.

45. For an excellent study of the war damage to Iran's economy, based on official statistics from the Iranian government, see Hooshang Amirahmadi, "War Damage and Reconstruction in the Islamic Republic of Iran," Amirahmadi and Parvin, *Post-Revolutionary Iran*, 126–152. Also, "Iran's War Loss Put at Trillion," *Washington Times*, January 7, 1990, p. A2.

46. On the earthquake damage, see "Quake Damage Exceeds $7,000 Million," *MEED* 34, no. 27 (July 13, 1990).

47. See *Iran Yearbook 1989/90*, 10–15.

48. On the statement by religious leaders on the necessity of birth control, see "Birth Control Campaign Launched," *MEED* 33, no. 1 (January 13, 1989).

49. On unemployment figures, see the statement by the Welfare Organization, *Iran Focus* 3, no. 11 (December 1990): 3; also, *Iran Yearbook 1989/90*, 17-7.

50. Official government estimates put the number of addicts at 1 million. But private estimates put the number much higher. See "In Last 6 Months, 40,000 Addicts Reportedly Arrested," *London Keyhan*, August 24, 1989, and "Committee Commander on Drug Enforcement," *FBIS/NEA*, November 5, 1989, p. 47.

51. On the history of foreign concessions in Iran and their negative political fallouts, see Ibrahim Teymouri, *Asr-e-Bikha bari Ya Tarikh-e-Imtiyazat dar Iran* (The era of ignorance or the history of concessions in Iran) (Tehran: Chap-e-Eghbal, 1332 [1953–1954]).

52. On World Bank emergency lending to Iran, see "World Bank to Provide Emergency Quake Loan," *MEED* 34, no. 38 (September 28, 1990): 14, and *MEED* 34, no. 42 (October 26, 1990): 12. Also see "The Future for the Iranian Economy," *MEED* 35, no. 45 (November 15, 1991).

53. On government policy on the sale of private industries, see *Iran Focus* 3, no. 10 (November 1990). According to the publication, Iran's finance and economic affairs minister, in a meeting with expatriate Iranian experts, traders, and businessmen in New York on September 29, 1990, said that a presidential committee is considering whether to return to the private sector or to close 800 state-controlled manufacturing and industrial concerns. Discussion on this issue predates Rafsanjani's administration. See "Privatization Plan Unveiled," *MEED* 33, no. 18 (May 12, 1989): 13.

54. On plans for Qishm Island, see *MidEast Report* 23, no. 20 (October 15, 1990): 16–18. The island will be linked to the mainland by a bridge. Another free trade zone is planned for Kish Island.

55. On the repairs to Abadan oil refinery, see *MEED* 32, no. 41 (October 14, 1988): 19. On the resumption of refining operations, see *MEED* 33, no. 7 (February 2, 1989): 21; also, "Rapid Recovery in Iran's War-Ravaged Oil Industry," *MEED* 33, no. 8 (March 3, 1989): 2–4.

56. On Tabriz and Shiraz refineries, see *MEED Special Report on Iran* (May 26, 1989): 12–14.

57. On exchange rate problems, see "Monetary Reform on the Way," *Iran Focus* 3, no. 6 (June 1990): 9–10; also see "Iran: Official Exchange Rate Fades Away," *MEED* 35, no. 44 (November 8, 1991).

58. On the Japanese interest, see "Liberal Breeze Warms Attitude toward Iran," *Japan Economic Journal* 28, no. 1445 (December 15, 1990): 11–12.

59. On Alviri's comments, see "Alviri Requests $4,800 Million Set Aside for Consumer Imports," *MEED* 33, no. 33 (August 25, 1989): 18.

60. See the text of the plan approved by the Majlis.

61. On visits by IMF and World Bank officials, see *MEED* 34, no. 42 (October 26, 1990): 14. The IMF's initial assessment of Iran's economic outlook was cautiously optimistic. See "Islamic

Republic of Iran Undergoes Profound Institutional, Structural Reform," *IMF Survey* 19, no. 15 (July 30, 1990): 226–229.

62. On French fund-raising efforts, see *MEED* 34, no. 48 (December 7, 1990): 29.

63. On oil and gas plans, see *MEED*'s special review of Iran's 16th International Trade Fair, October 1–10, 1990, as well as various issues of *MEED* and *Iran Focus* for 1990.

64. For industrial ventures, see ibid., 11–12.

65. The French are involved in the Tehran underground railway network. The first two lines of the network are due to start in 1992. The French may also become involved in building a similar network for Mashhad, the capital of Khorason Province. Ibid, 13. The Soviet republic of Azerbaijan has reached agreement on an underground railway network for Tabriz in the northwest. See *MEED* 34, no. 48 (December 7, 1990): 28.

66. See *MEED Special Report*, 14.

67. On Iran's cultural legacy, see A. J. Arberry, ed., *The Legacy of Persia* (Oxford: Clarendon Press, 1953).

68. On the negative effects of the antinationalist campaign on Iran's prestige, see Ali Moussavi Gharmaroudi "Negahi Be Iran Shenassi Baadaz Englab-e-Islami" (A look at Iranian studies after the Islamic revolution), *Seyasat-e-Khareji* (Foreign policy), no. 3 (Shahrivar 1367 [September 1988]). The important point is that this journal is published by the Foreign Ministry's Institute for Political and International Studies.

69. On the Islamic cultural revolution, see Farhang Rajaee, "The Islamic Cultural Revolution and Post-revolutionary Iranian Society," in Shireen T. Hunter, ed., *Internal Developments in Iran* (Washington, D.C.: Center for Strategic and International Studies, 1985), 49–61.

70. For more extensive discussion of these issues, see Shireen T. Hunter, *Iran and the World: Continuity in a Revolutionary Decade* (Bloomington, Ind.: Indiana University Press, 1990).

71. The statement by the then-president of Iran, Hodjat-al-Islam Khamenei, to the visiting West German foreign minister about Iran's humiliation at the hands of the great powers in the last two centuries illustrates this point. See *FBIS/SA*, July 24, 1984, I-3, I-4.

72. On Soviet-Iranian relations, see the relevant chapter in Hunter, *Iran and the World*, and R. K. Ramazani, *Iran's Foreign*

Relations 1941–1973 (Charlottesville: University of Virginia Press, 1973); also, Shireen T. Hunter, "The Soviet Union and the Islamic Republic of Iran," *Soviet-American Relations with Pakistan, Iran, and Afghanistan*, Hafeez Malik, ed. (New York: St. Martin's Press, 1987), 244–266, and Shahram Chubin and Sepehr Zabih, *The Foreign Relations of Iran* (Berkeley: University of California Press, 1979).

73. On Iran's oil diplomacy, see Shireen T. Hunter, *OPEC and the Third World: The Politics of Aid* (Bloomington, Ind.: Indiana University Press, 1985), 106–123.

74. Ibid., 117–123.

75. On the popular discontent on the misuse of oil money, see Shahram Chubin, "Local Soil, Foreign Plants," *Foreign Policy*, no. 34 (Spring 1979), particularly the following passage: "Few [Iranians] understood why a $10 billion defense budget had become a necessity overnight or why a war on the Horn of Africa threatened them. Nor could the majority of Iranians understand why large loans were being made to other countries when Iran's own countryside was deteriorating [p. 22]."

76. On radical Arab, especially Palestinian, subversion of Iran, see Jerold Green, *Revolution in Iran: The Politics of Countermobilization* (New York: Praeger, 1982), 127–128.

77. Hunter, *Iran and the World*, 36–45.

78. Ibid., 35–40.

79. This is one reason the United States has tried to spread liberal democratic ideas and the Soviet Union has tried to surround itself with socialists. Different Arab regimes have tried to do the same.

80. On similarities between the Bakhtiar and Bazargan governments' foreign policy postures, see Shahpour Bakhtiar's interview reprinted in *FBIS/ME & NA*, January 15, 1979, pp. R5–7, and the comments of Karim Snajabi, Iran's first postrevolution foreign minister in *FBIS/ME & NA*, February 5, 1979, p. R16.

81. This is best reflected in the following comment by the then-secretary general of the Tudeh Party, Noureddin Kianouri, "As long as the hostages are in Iran, normalization of relations with the United States . . . will not be possible." See *Le Monde*, April 18, 1980, p. 5.

82. The following commentary by Bani-Sadr in his journal "Englab-e-Islami" in August 1979 regarding Iran's role in Lebanon illustrates this point: " . . . by not paying attention to what is

happening there we will not be helping the advancement of our
revolution. . . . If we don't go out of Iran to help the revolution,
others will come to our country to plot against us. . . . " Quoted in
Sad Magaleh [One hundred essays], a collection of Bani-Sadr's
articles published by the Organization of Iranian Students in the
United States, 1358 (1979), 84.

83. See Richard W. Cottam, *Iran and the United States*
(Pittsburgh, Pa.: University of Pittsburgh Press, 1988).

84. For example, the one-time Iranian prosecutor-general,
Hodjat-al-Islam Khoeiniha—whom the French dubbed the "Red
Mullah"—served as liaison between the Tudeh Party and the religious opposition. Also, after the ascendancy of the radicals in
1981–1983 and the Tudeh infiltration into the Iranian military
and bureaucracy, the latter hoped to seize power through this
cooperation. See "Red Plot Sparks Off Anti-Russian Frenzy," *London Sunday Times*, May 8, 1983, p. 18.

85. On this aspect of Soviet-Iranian relations, see Hunter,
Iran and the World, 85–89; also Shireen T. Hunter, "Soviet-Iranian
Relations in the Post-Revolution Period," in R. K. Ramazani, ed.,
Iran's Revolution: The Search for Consensus (Bloomington: Indi-
ana University Press, 1990), 85–103.

86. See Hunter, *Iran and the World*, 144, 156.

87. See Gary Sick, "What Do We Think We Are Doing in the
Gulf?" *Washington Post*, April 24, 1988, p. D1.

88. On the lack of urgency to improve ties with Iran, see
"U.S.: Diplomatic Ball Is in Tehran's Court," *Christian Science
Monitor*, June 13, 1989, pp. 1–2. The view that Iran is not very
important predates the dramatic events of 1987–1988. See Freder-
ick W. Axelgard, "Mistaken Nostalgia about Iran," *Christian Science Monitor*, November 21, 1986, p. 20.

89. On the Ayatollah Amoli's visit to Moscow, see "Khomeini
Aides Meet with Gorbachev," *Washington Post*, January 5, 1989,
p. A27.

90. At one point, for example, when Iraqi missiles and bomb-
ers were daily hitting Iranian cities, Hodjat-al-Islam Rafsanjani
said that the Iranians would not forget that it was Soviet weapons that were killing Iranian children.

91. On Gorbachev's warning to Iran not to interfere in the
crisis in Azerbaijan, see *FBIS/NES*, January 12, 1990, p. 35; for
the *Tehran Times'* rejection of "taking advantage" of Soviet domestic problems and Foreign Minister Velayati's message to

Eduard Shevardnadze, which pledged "noninterference in the internal affairs of others" and called for "an immediate end to the crisis through peaceful means," see *FBIS/NES*, January 26, 1990, p. 32. Also see *MEED* 34, no. 41 (October 19, 1990): 38, on Syria's linkage between a reestablishment of British-Syrian relations and the release of British hostages in Lebanon.

92. On President Rafsanjani's comments, see "Hashemi Rafsanjani Ready to Help in Lebanon," *FBIS/MESA*, August 4, 1989, p. 43.

93. On Syria's role, see "Al-Shar Links British Hostages, Diplomatic Ties," *FBIS/NES*, October 19, 1990, pp. 42–43.

94. Even during the war, Iran's relations with some Persian Gulf countries such as Oman and the United Arab Emirates (UAE) and even Qatar were reasonably good.

95. See "Foreign Ministry Issues Statement on Arab Summit," *FBIS/NES*, June 1, 1990, pp. 23–24.

96. On the politics of quake relief, see "Relief Becomes a Political Battleground," *Iran Focus* 3, no. 7 (July–August 1990): 3–4. See also *FBIS/NES* issues during June and July, especially "Hashemi Rafsanjani Gives Sermon on Earthquake Aid," July 2, 1990, pp. 45–49.

97. On contacts between Iran and Kuwaiti officials since the Iraqi invasion, see "Kuwaiti Foreign Minister Meets Hashemi-Rafsanjani," *FBIS/NES*, August 24, 1990, p. 59.

98. On Iran's contacts with Yemen, see "Yemeni Foreign Minister Al-Iryani Visits," *FBIS/NES*, November 21, 1990, pp. 62–63.

99. On Iran's view on Persian Gulf security, see "Tehran Presses Claims as Gulf Protector," *Financial Times*, December 27, 1990, p. 3. Also, "Iran: Gulf States Offered 'Stable Anchor,'" *MEED* 34, no. 49 (December 14, 1990): 13.

100. On the GCC's new attitude toward Iran, see "Gulf Leaders Edge towards Iran," *Financial Times*, December 24, 1990, p. 3.

101. Robert Mauther, "Syria Firmly Opposed to Its 'Defensive' Force Operating inside Iraq," *Financial Times*, February 7, 1991, p. 2.

102. Carol Berger, "Arab Ministers Discuss Regional Pact for Security, Economic Cooperation," *Christian Science Monitor*, March 6, 1991, p. 4. For additional details, see also Carol Berger, "Egypt Pulls Out of Regional Force," *Christian Science Monitor*, May 9, 1991, p. 3.

103. Issam Hamza, "Syria Endorses Iranian Role in Gulf Security," *Washington Post*, April 29, 1991, p. A17.

104. On Velayati's trip to France, see *FBIS/NES*, December 6, 1990, and subsequent issues, including *FBIS/NES*, December 10, 1990, pp. 52–53, and *FBIS/NES*, December 11, 1990, pp. 49–50.

105. Jacques Amalric, "Un Prochain Sommet Scellera la Réconciliation Franco-Iranienne," *Le Monde*, May 5–6, 1991, pp. 1, 5; see also, "Meets with Hashemi-Rafsanjani," in *FBIS/NES*, May 6, 1991, p. 61.

106. "Genscher Describes Meetings" in *FBIS/NES*, May 7, 1991, p. 61.

Index

Afghanistan, Soviet invasion of, 47, 53–54, 111
Agricultural sector, 56; economy and, 68–69; five-year plan and, 91; shah and, 57–58
Algiers agreement of 1975, 126
Aluminum production, 90
Alviri, Morteza, 86
Amoli, Ayatollah Javadi, 120
Arab-Israeli peace process, 134
Arab League summit (May 30, 1990), 125
Arab nationalism, 11
Armenia, 122
Arms embargo, 117
Artistic expression, 92, 95–97
As-Sadr, Ayatollah Muhammad Baqir, 62
Assembly of Experts, 24, 26
Azerbaijan, 122

Bahrain: relations with, 130; U.S. security agreement with, 133
Baker, James, 130
Bakhtiar, Shahpour, 109
Bani-Sadr, Abol-Hassan, 47, 59, 110–11

Bazargan, Mehdi, 34, 108, 109–10
Birth control, 75
Black market, 70, 78–79
Brain drain, 43, 72, 100
Britain: encroachments in Persian Gulf, 9; hostages and, 124, 136; relations with, 135–36; Rushdie affair and, 124, 135; withdrawal from Persian Gulf, 103
Bureaucratic reform, 41–43, 86
Bush, George, 120–21, 137
Business community, confidence of, 43, 81–82, 83

Capital: flight of, 43, 64; shortage of, 76–78, 81
Carter, Jimmy, 105
Central Treaty Organization (CENTO), 109
Chess playing, 22
Ciccipio, Joseph, 123
Classless society, 58, 59
Clerical political groups, 23
Clerics, see Religious leaders
Consensus system of government, 31
Constitution: 1906, 6–7, 10, 28;

1979, 14–18, 19, 23–25, 47–48; 1989 reforms, 17–18, 21, 24–28
Consumer goods, shortages of, 80, 82
Consumption, 56
Cooper, Roger, 135
Copper production, 90
Council for the Reappraisal of the Constitution of the Islamic Republic of Iran, 24–28
Council of Discerning What Is Good, 25
Council of Guardians (or Guardian Council), 22, 27, 64
Coup attempts, 46
Cultural purification, 10
Culture: identity and, 8–13, 140–41; Iranian component of, 17; Islamizing, 92–98; political system and, 6–14
Currency speculation, 65, 70, 79, 83

Damascus Declaration, 131, 132
Dam building, 68, 77
Defense policy, 33. *See also* Military
Dress code, 71
Drug addiction, 76

Earthquake (June 21, 1990), 74, 77, 125–26
Economic boycott, 111
Economic development: first five-year plan and, 65–67; framework for, 58–59; second five-year plan and, 75, 84–89; self-reliant, 59–60; social needs and, 21, 60
Economic gap, 69–71
Economic reconstruction, shortage of mid-level experts and, 42
Economy, 37, 56–91, 143; agriculture and, 68–69; capital shortage and, 76–78; confusing signals and, 63–64; current characteris-

tics of, 67–74; deterioration of, 43; egalitarian, 59; growth rate, 82, 86; ideological confusion and, 58–61; industrial stagnation and, 71–72; Iran-Iraq War and, 65, 66, 72–74; Islamic system, 59, 61–65; oil dependence and, 67; popular committees and, 64–65; prospects for, 74–80; Rafsanjani administration and, 80–91; regional disparities and, 72; revolutionary institutions and, 64–65; shah and, 56–58; state role in, 60–65; war damage and, 72–74
Education, 69, 98–100
Egalitarianism, 59, 62, 98
Egypt: relations with, 132; U.S. and, 137
Electronic media, encouraging, 95–97
Emulation, sources of, 19, 25–26
Entrepreneurs, flight of, 64
Ethnic unrest, 47
Europe, Iran's relations with, 135
European Community: relations with, 124, 135; Rushdie affair and, 119
Exchange rate, 79, 82–84
Executive power, 23, 28–31
Exiles, 38, 42–43
Experts, exodus of, 99
Export earnings, 67
Expropriation, 70

Factionalism, chronic, 4
Fedayan-e-Khalq, 46, 112
Federal Republic of Germany: earthquake assistance and, 125; ties with, 119
Fiat, 90
Film industry, 96
Food imports, 56, 68
Foreign debt, 76–77, 80, 85
Foreign exchange earnings, 56, 67, 83

Foreign investment, 78, 85, 88–89
Foreign relations, 101–38; activist
policy, 103–4; after the revolution, 106–38; Bani-Sadr presidency and, 110–11; Bazargan
government and, 109–10; Islamic principles and, 107; Khamenei
and, 40; moderates and, 37; national interest and, 136; 1979,
102–6; 1981–1984, 112–14; 1984–
1988, 114–21; pro-Soviet tilt,
112–13; radicals and, 38–39; Rafsanjani and, 121–26; regional
politics and, 131–35; transitional
period, 109–12
Foreign trade, 38, 138
France: earthquake assistance
and, 125; Iran-Iraq War and,
114; relations with, 124–25, 136

Geopolitical position, 101
Ghotbzadeh, Sadegh, 110, 112
God, political legitimacy and, 14,
21
Gorbachev, Mikhail, 122
Government, need for profession-
als in, 41–43
Gross domestic product, 66
Gross national product, 56, 86
Guardian Council, 22, 27, 64
Gulf Cooperation Council, 131,
133

Hafiz Shirazi, 95
Haft-e-Tir International Airport,
90
Handicapped, Iran-Iraq War and,
73
Heavy industry, 57
Hostage crisis, 134–37
Housing prices, 79
Human rights, 45
Hurd, Douglas, 131
Hussein, Saddam, 127, 128, 129,
132

Ijtihad, 22
Illiteracy, 69
Imam, return of the twelfth,
19
Import dependency, 71
Income distribution, 56, 58, 69–
70, 84
India, Soviet Union and, 103
Industrial and Scientific Research
Organization, 100
Industrialization, 56, 57
Industrial production, 80
Industrial revolution, 9–10
Industrial stagnation, 71–72
Inflation, 66, 78–79, 82
Insurgencies, 43–44
Intellectuals: exodus of, 99; nation-
alism and, 10–11; social needs
and, 60
Internal security instruments, re-
form of, 43–45
International Monetary Fund, 77,
88, 126
Iran-contra affair, 36–37, 117
Iranian Islam, 17, 95, 140–41
Iranianism, relegitimization of, 94–
95
Iran-Iraq War, 2, 47, 48, 54; economy and, 65, 66, 72–74; France
and, 114; nationalism and, 17,
93–94; oil production and, 67;
power struggles in Iran and, 111;
psychological impact of, 73–74;
Revolutionary Guards and, 51–
52; United States and, 113,
117
Iraq: embargo against, 85, 128; invasion of Kuwait, 126–32; peace
with, 127–30; Shi'a-populated areas of, 36; Soviet activities in,
102; United States support for,
113
Irrigation, 68
Islam: Iranian culture and, 8–13;
1906 constitution and, 6–7

Islamic Consultative Assembly, 25

Islamic economic system, 59, 61–65

Islamic law, 7, 64; different legal schools and, 21; Guardian Council and, 22; judicial system and, 31–32; nature of, 21–23; 1979 constitution and, 14–15; supreme religious leader and, 18–20; will of God and, 21

Islamic moral code, 37, 38

Islamic nationalists, 108

Islamic political order, ideal, 2

Islamic principles: foreign relations and, 107; interpretation of, 22

Islamic reform, attacked by hardliners, 23

Islamic regime: arts and, 95–97; cultural philosophy, 92–98; education and, 98–100

Islamic theocracy, 15, 16

Israel: peace process and, 134; ties with, 104,

Italy, ties with, 124–25

Ja'afari school of twelver Shi'ism, 7

Jordan, diplomatic relations with, 132

Judiciary, composition of, 31–32

Karubi, Ayatollah Mehdi, 26–27, 40

Khalkhali, Ayatollah Sadeq, 27, 35, 128

Khamenei, Hodjat-al-Islam Ali, 24, 26, 27, 30, 31, 40, 94, 115, 128

Khomeini, Ahmad, 40–41

Khomeini, Ayatollah Ruhollah, 1; constitutional basis for leadership, 19; death of, 3, 121; economy and, 59, 64; foreign policy and, 115; health of, 20; Islamic vision, 2; moderate-radical power shifts and, 114; monarchy and, 16; nationalism and, 16; overwhelming influence of, 108–9; poetry of, 95; power of Ijtihad, 22; radicals and, 39; regime's successes and, 2–3; Rushdie affair and, 119; as source of law, 21; successor to, 20, 25–26

Khusistan, 47, 127, 139

Kowkabi, Mehrdad, 135

Kurdish refugees, 135, 139–40

Kuwait: Iraq's invasion of, 126–32; U.S. security agreement with, 133

Landownership regime, 68–69

Land reform, 38, 62, 64, 69

Law and order, reestablishment of, 43–45

Lawyers, right to representation by, 45

Lebanon: hostages in, 136–37; subversive activities in, 113, 114

Leftist forces, power struggle and, 112

Leftist ideologies, Islam and, 62–63

Literary figures, rehabilitation of, 95

Living standards, 56, 58, 69, 70, 104

Lower classes, Islamic economics and, 63

Managerial talent, shortages of, 42, 64, 86

Medical professionals, 42

Merchant class, Islamic economics and, 63, 64

Military, 46–55; background, 46–49; buildup of, 103–4, 105; commander in chief of, 40; conse-

Military (*continued*)
quences of antagonizing, 54; expenditures on, 53–54; Iranian society and politics and, 50–53; Islamic indoctrination, 47; loyalties of, 49; mergers and, 48–49; political differences within, 51, 52–53; purges and, 47; religious leadership and, 51; shah and, 53; size of, 53–55; Soviet supplies to, 54, 120
Military industrial base, 55
Mineral resources, 80, 90
Ministry of Justice, 32
Ministry of the Interior, law enforcement and, 44
Moderate-radical dichotomy, 35–41
Modernization, disenchantment with, 11
Mohtashami, Hodjat-al-Islam, 35, 123, 128
Monarchy, 7; cult of, 12; Khomeini and, 16
Montazeri, Ayatollah Hossein Ali, 20
Months, names of, 16
Mossadegh, Mohammad, 14, 109
Moussavi, Hossein, 84–85
Mujaheddin-e-Khalq, 13, 46, 112
Mujtahid, 31, 32
Music, 22, 95–96

National Consultative Assembly, 25
Nationalism, 141; Ayatollah Khomeini and, 16; early 1900s, 10–11; Iran-Iraq War and, 17, 93–94; Islamic, 9, 108; military and, 51; moderates and, 38; Pahlavis and, 7–8, 11–12, 17; Persian, 92; secular, 6, 16, 108, 109
Nationalization, 64, 70, 78
National Research Council, 100
Nixon doctrine, 103

Obeid, Shaykh Abd-al-Karim, 123
Oil, 66; dependency on revenues from, 56, 57; economy and, 67; exports of, 85, 87; prices, 80, 85–86, 87–88, 104, 106; war damage and, 72–73
Oil and gas output, 89
Oil and gas reserves, 76
Oil industry, repair of, 80–81
Oil revolution of 1973, 106
Oil wealth, waste of, 57
Oman: mediation efforts and, 125; relations with, 130
Open-door policy, 115
Organization of Petroleum Exporting Countries (OPEC), 104

Pahlavi, Mohammad Reza (Shah of Iran): agriculture and, 57–58; arrogance of, 104; economic policy, 56–58; industrialization and, 57; military and, 53; security and, 103, 106; Soviet Union and, 102–3
Pahlavi, Reza Shah, 6, 7–8
Pahlavi family: cultural policy, 8; education and, 98; military and, 50–51; nationalism and, 7–8, 11–12, 17; religious establishment and, 7–8, 12–13; secularizing policies of, 92
Palestinian problem, 128
Parliament: Islamic law and, 21; Muslim clerics and, 7; president and, 29–30, 33; radicals and, 40, 64; role of, 22; supreme religious leader and, 30
Parliamentary-style executive, 29
People-to-people relations, 108, 114, 115
Persian Gulf, U.S. presence in, 5, 54, 117
Persian Gulf crisis, 4–5, 126–32; embargo against Iraq and, 85, 128; moderates and, 35–36; oil

prices and, 87–88; U.S. moderation of military arrangements and, 54–55
Persian culture, 10, 16, 17, 38
Persian language, 10, 94
Persian music, 96, 97
Persian nationalism, 92–94
Persianness, 12
Personal freedoms, constitutional limitations on, 7
Peugeot, 90
Polhill, Robert, 124
Political associations, 22–23
Political parties, 22
Politics: cultural foundations, 6–14; military role in, 50–53
Population growth, 56, 67, 68, 74–75, 87, 99
Populism, 59
Poster art, 96
Power generation, 89–90
President: Parliament and, 29–30, 33; role of, 23–24, 29–31
Presidential-style executive, 29
Prime minister: elimination of post, 32–33; role of, 23–24, 29
Private investment, 81
Private sector, Rafsanjani and, 81–82
Professionalism, need for, 41–43
Property rights, 37, 61, 68–69
Provinces, economic development and, 58
Publishing, encouraging, 95–97
Purification campaign, 42

Qatar, relations with, 134
Qur'an, 14, 21

Radicals, 27, 34; Parliament and, 40, 64; return of professionals and, 42; Rushdie affair and, 119
Radio, 25, 97
Rafsanjani, Ali Akbar Hashemi, 4, 22, 29, 30, 144; bureaucratic

reform and, 42; economy and, 70, 80–91; education and, 100; five-year development plan and, 84–89; foreign country visits, 115; foreign policy and, 121–26; historic monuments and, 94; military command and, 48; moderate-radical dichotomy and, 39–41; Moscow visit, 120, 121–22; Persian Gulf War and, 35; private sector and, 81–82; Syrian visit, 132; U.S. and, 122–23
Rastakhiz party, 8
Real estate speculation, 65, 70
Recreational facilities, 76
Reed, Frank, 124
Refugees, Iran-Iraq War and, 73, 135, 139–40
Regional security, 131–33, 137, 141
Religious establishment: corrupt elite and, 11; Iranian culture and, 93; Pahlavis and, 12–13. *See also* Religious leaders
Religious groups, ideological divisions and, 13–14
Religious leader, supreme, 18–20, 30, 25–27, 49
Religious leaders: economics and, 62–63; guardianship of the supreme and, 18–20, 25–27; military and, 51; 1906 constitution and, 7; 1979 constitution and, 15–16, 18; Pahlavis and, 7–8; population control and, 75; qualifications of, 25–27; rich families and, 62; selection of, 19, 20; sources of emulation, 19, 25–26
Resalat Foundation, 23
Research and development, 100
Revolution, exporting, 2, 39, 107–8, 113–14
Revolution of 1979, 8, 13–14, 46, 50
Revolutionary Guards, 38, 39, 47–50, 51, 54

Revolutionary leaders, legitimacy of, 20
Revolutionary organizations, activities of, 44
Rich class, 70
Rural areas: neglect of, 58; social infrastructure and, 69
Rushdie, Salman, 118–19, 124, 135
Russo-Iranian wars, 9

Safavid period (1502–1736), 9
Satanic Verses (Rushdie), 118–19
Saudi Arabia: international forces in, 127, 129, 130; relations with, 131, 132, 133; U.S.-Iran relations and, 116
Scientific advancement, 10
Secularization: disenchantment with, 11; 1800s, 10
Secular left, 112
Secular nationalism, 6, 16, 108, 109
Security Guard Corps, 44–45
Security environment, congenial, 108
Shah of Iran, *see* Pahlavi, Mohammad Reza
Shariati, Ali, 62
Shat-al-Arab, 126
Shevardnadze, Eduard, 120
Shi'a Islam, 9, 27–28
Shi'a theory of government, 15–16, 18–20
Social inequalities, 58, 61, 69–71
Socialism, religious leaders and, 62–63
Socialist systems, collapse of, 38
Social justice, 21, 62, 143
Social needs, economic growth vs., 60
Social programs, funds for, 53
Society, military role in, 50–53
South Africa, ties with, 104, 109
Soviet Union: Asian republics, 122; Bani-Sadr and, 110; cooperation with, 85; India and, 103; invasion of Afghanistan, 53–54, 111; Iranian revolution and, 112; military supplies from, 54, 120; Rafsanjani's trip to, 120, 121–22; relations with, 37, 102–3, 107, 119, 121; shah and, 102–3
Sports, lack of, 76
Stagflation, 79
Steel production, 90
Supreme Council for Support of the War Effort, 48
Supreme Court, 31
Supreme Defense Council, 47–48, 51
Supreme Judicial Council, 31
Supreme National Security Council, 33
Syria: hostage problem and, 124; Persian Gulf crisis and, 128; ties with, 132

Taxation, Islamic system of, 61, 69–70
Teaching profession, 99
Technical expertise, shortages of, 42, 86
Technocrats, 41
Technology: imports of, 71; self-sufficiency and, 100
Tehran Militant Clerics, 23
Tehran Militant Clergy Association, 23
Television, 25, 97
Territorial losses, 101
Terrorism, 107, 116
Theater, 96–97
Theology Teachers' Association, 23
Third World countries: economies of, 56; Iran's image among, 104; ties with, 107
Third World intellectuals, 59–60
Tourism industry, 94
Transcaucasian provinces, 9
Transport network, 90–91

Tribal unrest, 47
Tudeh Party, 13, 112, 113
Tunisia, diplomatic relations with, 132
Turkey: nationalism and, 11; U.S. and, 137

Umat-al-Islam, 16, 95
Unemployment, 74, 75–76, 86
United Arab Emirates: relations with, 130; U.S. security agreement with, 133
United Nations Security Council Resolution 598, 117, 125, 127, 129
United States: Bazargan government and, 110; exaggerating Iranian threat and, 137; hostages and, 110–11, 123–24, 136–37; Iran-Iraq War and, 117; Iran's military buildup and, 105; Khamenei and, 40; military information to, 49; moderates and, 37; in Persian Gulf, 5, 117; Persian Gulf policy and, 113; radicals and, 38; Rafsanjani and, 122–23;

relations with, 102, 120–21, 136, 137; trade with, 138
Urbanization, 56, 58

Velayat-e-Faqih, 19–20, 28
Velayati, Ali-Akbar, 39
Vice presidents, 33

Waite, Terry, 124
Wealth, accumulation of, 38
West: contact with, 9–10; earthquake assistance and, 125; economic dependence on, 59–60; Iran's military buildup and, 105; opening up toward, 118; Rushdie affair and, 119; security policy and, 103; ties with, 37, 128
Western culture, fascination with, 98
Will of the nation, 14–15
World Bank, 77, 88, 126

Yemen, relations with, 131
Youth, leftist ideas and, 63

Zoroastrian angels, 16